BLACK JACK

America's Famous Riderless Horse

ROBERT KNUCKLE

Published by

GENERAL STORE
PUBLISHING HOUSE

Box 28, 1694B Burnstown Road, Burnstown, Ontario, Canada K0J 1G0
Telephone (613) 432-7697 or 1-800-465-6072

ISBN 1-894263-65-0
Printed and bound in Canada

Design layout by Derek McEwen
Cover Design by Brian Murray
Printing by Custom Printers of Renfrew Ltd.

National Library of Canada Cataloguing in Publication Data

Knuckle, Robert, 1935-
    Black Jack : America's Famous Riderless Horse / Robert Knuckle.

ISBN 1-894263-65-0

    1. Black Jack (Horse) 2. War horses—United States—Biography. I. Title.

UC603.K58 2002   973.92'092'9   C2002-902534-6

Second Printing July 2003

This book is dedicated to Alexander James Barthorpe,
our newest grandson.

CONTENTS

Preface

This book was initiated by a visit I made to the caisson stables of the 3rd U.S. Infantry Regiment (The Old Guard) at Fort Myer, Virginia, and a tour of Arlington National Cemetery, which is located adjacent to the fort. During my conversations with personnel at the stables, I was told about Black Jack and invited to browse through an interesting museum dedicated in his honor. Like many people, I was vaguely familiar with Black Jack and his participation in the funeral of President John F. Kennedy. But I had no idea of his long and remarkable career—one that makes him the most celebrated horse in the history of the U.S. Army.

The information at the museum whetted my interest in Black Jack and encouraged me to learn more about his life. Although there were many details and anecdotes available about Black Jack, I discovered there was no official written record of his long and meritorious service to the army and the nation.

Consequently, I began contacting people who either knew Black Jack or had served with him in The Old Guard Caisson Platoon at Fort Myer. My research clearly demonstrated that the story of Black Jack's career was amazing. Above all, the tale of Black Jack's life is the classic success story of a common and cantankerous cavalry mount who went on to achieve international fame.

The wondrous details of Black Jack's life and his accomplishments are in the book you are about to read.

CHAPTER ONE

November 1963

BLACK JACK wasn't always famous. In fact, he began his life as a simple cavalry horse and was quite old before he became a celebrity. The pivotal point in his career occurred in 1963 when he was chosen to serve as the riderless horse in the funeral procession of John F. Kennedy. Ever since then Black Jack's name and fame have been inextricably connected with that tragically memorable event.

There is more to Black Jack's life than that, but the best way to begin his story is to revisit those awful days in November 1963 when John Kennedy died and was buried. The people who lived through those times will never forget them; those who did not can benefit from a review of that episode in history.

On Friday, November 22, the first alarming news from Texas alerted the nation and the world that the president had been shot while riding in a motorcade in downtown Dallas. For a brief time the disjointed news reports were confusing. It wasn't clear whether John F. Kennedy was slightly injured, badly wounded, or worse. People everywhere rushed to their radios and televisions for more information. Comments from Dallas reporters and a number of witnesses at the scene did not sound good. Still, everyone continued to hope and pray that the president's wounds were not mortal. Shortly after 2:30 p.m., EST, their hopes were dashed when venerable CBS anchorman Walter Cronkite removed his glasses, pursed his lips, and with agony in his eyes announced in a trembling voice that President John F. Kennedy was dead.

From the time the president was shot until his casket was loaded aboard Air Force One in Dallas, Jacqueline Kennedy remained at her husband's side. Still dressed in her rose-colored, bloodstained suit, she left him only long enough to stand beside Lyndon Johnson on the airplane while the tall Texan took the presidential oath of office. Then Jackie returned to her place beside the casket for the painful flight back to Washington. From then on almost every detail and image of the next four days was captured by the media.

When the plane landed at Andrews Air Force Base, the rear cargo door opened to reveal Jackie standing there, holding her brother-in-law Robert Kennedy's hand. Their anguished eyes stared vacantly at the dark, red-bronze coffin as it was lowered on a yellow cargo lift and loaded into a gray service ambulance. With Jackie on board, the vehicle departed for Bethesda Naval Hospital where the president's body was prepared for burial. Early the next morning, the same navy ambulance carried the slain president home on his final trip to the White House.

Abraham Lincoln (1809–65), sixteenth president of the United States *U.S. National Archives*

John F. Kennedy (1917–63), thirty-fifth president of the United States *The John F. Kennedy Library, Boston*

Jacqueline Kennedy, in planning her husband's funeral, was guided by the principle that her husband "belongs to the people." Fascinated by the similarities between his death and the assassination of Abraham Lincoln, she requested that her husband's funeral rites be modeled on the ceremonies afforded Lincoln in 1865. In accordance with her wishes, two government officials were dispatched to the repository of the Library of Congress to research the details of Lincoln's funeral. In their research they determined that replicating some of those funeral arrangements would be possible, some would not.

Jackie was aware that the men of Lincoln's government were determined to make Lincoln's funeral the most memorable event in U.S. history. Jackie, with her keen sense of history, wanted an equally momentous series of ceremonies put in place for her husband Jack.

She learned that Lincoln's body had lain in state for two days in an open casket in the spacious East Room of the White House, his coffin resting atop an eleven-foot-high catafalque dubbed "The Temple of Doom." During those two days only government officials and visiting dignitaries were admitted to pay their respects. On the third day, Wednesday, April 19, 1865, Lincoln's funeral service was held in the East Room attended by some 600 distinguished guests, only seven of whom were women. Then, in a lengthy procession along Pennsylvania Avenue, Lincoln's casket was drawn to the Capitol by six horses pulling a fourteen-foot-long hearse that very much resembled a draped and decorated wagon. There was no riderless horse used in this procession.

On Thursday, the general public was allowed to file past Lincoln's body, which lay atop the "Temple of Doom" catafalque in an open coffin under the great dome of the Capitol rotunda.

The next day, Lincoln's casket and another containing his son Willie, who had died two years previously and had been interred in a Washington crypt, were put on board a nine-car funeral train. Accompanying them as escorts were some 300 high-ranking officials. The train and its entourage then commenced a 1,700-mile rail trip to the Lincoln crypt in Springfield, Illinois. En route Lincoln's coffin was off-loaded for mammoth funeral processions that were held on the streets of nine major cities including Philadelphia, New York, Buffalo, Cleveland, and Chicago. Each city in its turn organized spectacular cavalcades that featured numerous marching units following Lincoln's casket, which was displayed atop a variety of ornate horse-drawn hearses.

Only when the funeral train reached its final destination was the concept of a riderless horse introduced into the cortege. In Springfield, Abe Lincoln's horse, Old Bob, was brought out of pasture retirement and dressed in a black mourning blanket with white fringe and tassels to follow the hearse to the graveyard.

Jacqueline Kennedy decided that her husband's body, like Lincoln's, was to lie in state in the East Room of the White House for twenty-four hours. Under her direction, the White House staff set

Abraham Lincoln's funeral cortege in New York City, 1865   *PictureHistory.com*

out to transform the great salon so it resembled the room in Lincoln's time. In 1865, the huge chandeliers had been darkened with shrouds, and black drapes had covered the windows. In 1963 the three chandeliers were dimmed with thick bolts of crepe and black curtains were hung over the five large windows to block out the garish sunlight. Jackie also placed two kneeling benches beside her husband's closed, flag-draped coffin and positioned a dark blue rug leading to the casket. John Kennedy's catafalque was modelled on that of Lincoln's, except it was lower and less ornate.

Abraham Lincoln's caparisoned
horse, Old Bob, Springfield, Illinois,
1865   *PictureHistory.com*

In accordance with Jackie's wishes, on Saturday morning there was a private mass in the East Room for family members. Then, as the day wore on, many representatives from the government and a host of foreign dignitaries came to kneel beside the casket to pay their respects. All the while, an honor guard representing all branches of the armed forces stood in silent vigil beside their fallen commander-in-chief.

Because Jackie wanted her husband's grave accessible to the people, she decided to have him buried near Washington and not in the family plot at Holyhood Cemetery in his birthplace of Brookline, Massachusetts. This decision ruled out a train cavalcade like that in Lincoln's time.

To comply with Jackie's wishes that her husband be buried close to Washington, Secretary of Defense Robert McNamara was assigned to contact Jack Metzler, the superintendent of Arlington National Cemetery, to ascertain which potential burial plots were available in the hallowed military graveyard.

Arlington National Cemetery was an unexpected choice for interment because only one other president, William H. Taft, had been buried there and that occurred in 1930. However, it was a most appropriate selection because Jack Kennedy had served with distinction as a torpedo-boat commander in the Pacific during World War II.

Three sites at the cemetery were offered and shown to Robert Kennedy. He preferred the one on the slope in front of the Custis-Lee mansion because from that place there is a beautiful, panoramic view of Washington. The attorney general was aware that his brother Jack, on a recent visit to the cemetery, had stood on the hill near this same spot and remarked that the view of Washington from there was so magnificent that, "I could stay here forever."

When Jacqueline Kennedy was brought to the location for her approval, she readily concurred with Bobby's choice. To mark the grave as a national memorial for future generations, the young widow asked that an eternal flame be installed similar to that of the French Unknown Soldier in Paris. In accordance with her wishes, arrangements were made with the Washington Gas Company to connect a propane-fed torch over the grave.

John Kennedy's ceremonial processions were designed with an equally dramatic flair. The first of these occurred on Sunday, November 24, when his casket was borne on a flag-draped caisson from the White House to the Capitol in a military cortege dominated by the rhythmic thud of muffled drums. This same, dull, haunting cadence, repeated over and over, became the signature sound of his funeral.

Three pairs of matched gray horses pulled the caisson. They were ridden by soldiers of the president's own ceremonial unit known as The Old Guard. The horses, by long-established custom, were all saddled but only those on the left of each pair were ridden. The three pairs were escorted by a section sergeant astride another matching gray. Marching on either side of the caisson was the all-services casket team. Behind the caisson, a Navy Seaman carried the president's flag. Behind him came Black Jack, the riderless horse that was provided by The Old Guard ceremonial unit from nearby Fort Myer.

The addition of Black Jack was another touch of Jackie's flair for historical pageantry. She knew that a riderless horse was used in funerals in Arlington National Cemetery for high-ranking military officers. At the cemetery they referred to such a mount as a "caparisoned" horse, an antiquated term meaning a horse suitably adorned for ceremonial purposes. Such a caparisoned horse was used in George Washington's funeral rites. Furthermore, Jackie was aware that since the time of Genghis Khan, a riderless horse in a funeral cortege was the traditional symbol of a leader who would ride no more. In the research presented to her regarding Lincoln's funeral, she was

The caisson unit and Black Jack en route from the White House to the Capitol Building, November 24, 1963
The John F. Kennedy Library, Boston

impressed by the fact that Old Bob was used in the Springfield, Illinois, procession that carried Lincoln to his grave.

Since her husband, as the nation's commander-in-chief, was to be given a military funeral and was to be buried in Arlington National Cemetery, Jackie chose to have a caparisoned horse follow the caisson in all the funeral processions that were held over the next two days. From the moment she first saw Black Jack, she was impressed with his appearance.

He was beautiful, sleek and well-muscled, jet black in color with a small, white star on his forehead. Exquisitely groomed, even his hooves were polished. His black saddlecloth was trimmed in white, and a gleaming regimental sword dangled from his glistening saddle. As the symbol of a fallen leader, he carried spurred cavalry boots thrust backwards in the stirrups.

7

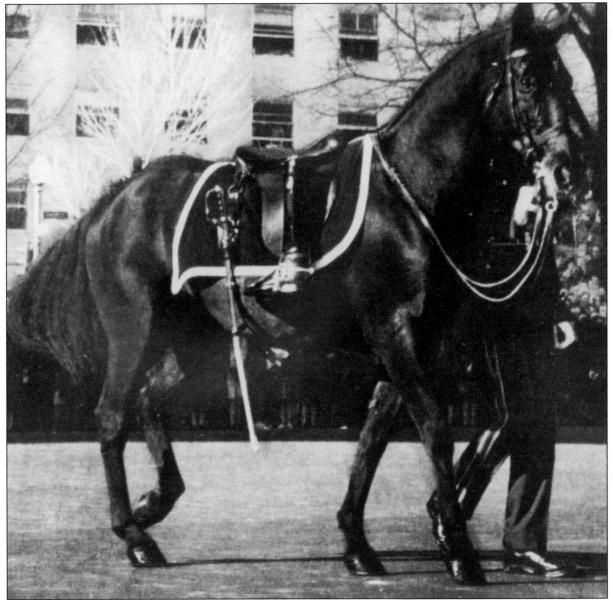

Black Jack marching in John F. Kennedy's funeral cortege   *The U.S. Army; courtesy of Nancy Schado*

Black Jack and his walker arriving with the caisson at the Capitol
The John F. Kennedy Library, Boston

At the Capitol, Black Jack waits for John Kennedy's coffin to be removed from the caisson. Robert Kennedy, Caroline, Jacqueline Kennedy, John-John, and Lyndon and Ladybird Johnson can be seen in the distance.
The John F. Kennedy Library, Boston

Black Jack's vitality was equally impressive. Every step of the way his head bobbed up and down as he energetically tugged on his walker's line. Often he pranced about in such a lively, spirited manner that sometimes he seemed to be walking sideways.

When the procession arrived at the Capitol, the all-services casket team carried the coffin up the thirty-six steps into the great rotunda while the navy band played John Kennedy's favored navy hymn, "Eternal Father Strong to Save."

Under the dome of the Capitol the coffin was placed on the catafalque brought from the East Room. Once again it had been modified so that it was less ornate and closer to the floor than in Lincoln's time. At 11:00 a.m. there was a special service attended by John Kennedy's family, his Cabinet, the Justices of the Supreme Court, senators, congressmen, members of the White House staff, and foreign diplomats. As the ritual unfolded, Jacqueline, her sad eyes hidden behind a dark veil, stood firm and erect holding the hands of her young children. Caroline would turn six in just three days; John-John was one day away from his third birthday.

At the conclusion of the service, the Capitol doors were opened to the public, who came by the hundreds of thousands. The biting November winds chilled by temperatures in the low thirties did not deter them. Many stood for hours—some all through the night—in lines that stretched two miles beyond the Capitol. All they wanted was a chance to say a brief goodbye to a man they loved. John Kennedy with his style and his wit had been so fresh and promising, like a beacon that pointed to a bright future with wonderful things to come. Now that light had gone out and America was stunned and stumbling in the dark.

On the day of the president's funeral, Jacqueline Kennedy, Caroline and John-John lead other members of the Kennedy family out of the Capitol Building, November 25, 1963
The John F. Kennedy Library, Boston

The funeral cortege moving from the Capitol to the White House, November 25, 1963
The John F. Kennedy Library, Boston

Monday, November 25, brought no respite from their distress. The day began with Jacqueline Kennedy retrieving her husband's body from the Capitol. Accompanied by her children, and Bobby and Ted Kennedy, she arrived at the rotunda at 10:40 a.m. and knelt at the casket one final time. Minutes later, the nine military pallbearers lifted her husband's coffin from the catafalque, carried it from the rotunda and placed it on a caisson at the foot of the Capitol steps. Black Jack waited restlessly and seemed relieved when the procession began to move forward. Once again his nervous energy kept him tugging and prancing sideways as the cortege sustained its measured movement toward the White House.

Behind Black Jack came seven limousines, the first of which carried Jackie, Caroline, John-John, and Bobby and Ted Kennedy.

As the cortege moved slowly away, it was soon joined at Constitution Avenue by units from the military services, cadets from the service academies, the Marine Band, the Navy Band and the Air Force Band. En route, each band took turns playing songs like "America the Beautiful" and hymns such as "Onward Christian Soldiers."

Once again the dominating sound of the procession was the steady cadence of the muffled drums and the constant crunch, crunch, crunch of marching feet. But it was the sight of noble, fiery Black Jack prancing vigorously behind the caisson that stirred the people's imagination and touched their hearts.

At the White House, Jackie left her children to ride in the limousine and made the unprecedented gesture of walking to the church behind the caisson and the caparisoned horse. Wearing a heavy black veil and stylish black suit, she walked between Bobby and Ted, the three of them keeping a brisk, determined pace behind Black Jack.

Following them came the greatest array of world leaders ever assembled in the United States. Kings, queens, princes, presidents, prime ministers, chancellors, and diplomats surged forth from under the portico of the White House and walked behind the Kennedys to the church. Although they marched more like a disorganized mob than an assembly of dignitaries, their participation was a powerful display of historic grandeur.

After the world leaders came the devastated young men of The New Frontier who had loved John Kennedy from the start, who had worked and fought for him, and had ridden to power and glory with him.

Newsmen marched too, wearing strange temporary credentials that read: "Trip of the president." The tags, issued in haste by White House officials, were obviously intended for a more joyous occasion.

Black Jack leading the funeral cortege from the White House to St. Matthew's Cathedral, November 25, 1963
The John F. Kennedy Library, Boston

Bobby, Jackie, and Ted Kennedy leading the dignitaries from the White House to St. Matthew's Cathedral
The John F. Kennedy Library, Boston

Charles de Gaulle, King Baudouin I of Belgium, and Haile Selassie in uniform at the head of the mourners walking to St. Matthew's Cathedral
The John F. Kennedy Library, Boston

Richard Cardinal Cushing meets John Kennedy's casket outside St. Matthew's Cathedral

The John F. Kennedy Library, Boston

For eight blocks the massive entourage plodded on, past hordes of reverent onlookers whose vigilance was alerted by the beat of the drums and stilled by the intermittent skirl of bagpipes and the deep toll of distant church bells.

When the procession arrived at St. Matthew's Cathedral, Jackie was joined by her children. All three went up the steps to be greeted by Richard Cardinal Cushing, a special friend of the family who had married Jacqueline and John Kennedy only ten years previously. The kindly old priest bent down and gently kissed Caroline on the cheek and patted John-John on the head.

After the coffin was removed from the caisson, Cardinal Cushing went down to street level to receive it and lead it into the church. As soon as the pallbearers carried it through the portal, the great bronze doors of the cathedral closed behind them.

Twelve hundred guests listened intently to the aged cardinal in his black vestments as he began the low requiem mass by intoning an ancient prayer in his raspy Boston accent:

Be merciful we beseech Thee, O Lord,
To the soul of Thy servant John Fitzgerald Kennedy
Whom you have just called out of this world . . .
He put his hope and trust in You. Do not then let him
Undergo the pains of hell, but bring him to happiness
Without end. . . . I am the resurrection and the life.
He who believes in Me, even if he die, shall live.

During the hour-long ceremony, Luigi Vena, a Boston tenor who had performed at the Kennedys' wedding, sang four solos, the most beautiful of which was a soaring rendition of Schubert's "Ave Maria."

When the mass was over, the cardinal came down from the high altar to bless the casket with holy water and incense and to bestow a final absolution on the mortal remains of America's first Roman Catholic president.

Then the pallbearers carried the casket down the cathedral steps and loaded it on the caisson for the final leg of its journey. It was then that John-John, standing beside his mother at the top of the steps, gave his famous little soldier's salute, perhaps the most moving moment of all during the poignant ceremony.

The procession from St. Matthew's to Arlington National Cemetery was composed of the same marching contingents as before, except now the mourners rode in limousines. Every ten yards along the route there was a service member posted on each side of the street. Each of them rippled to attention as the caisson passed by. With the drums keeping their relentless cadence, the long cortege was soon on the bridge crossing the Potomac, with the Custis-Lee mansion in sight atop the hill ahead.

When the cortege neared the entrance to the cemetery, the ceremonial troops turned away while the caisson and Black Jack continued into Arlington National Cemetery towards the gravesite on the slope of the hill.

Black Jack and the seven matched grays stood and waited on the roadway while the coffin was removed from the caisson and the Air Force Pipers played "Mist Covered Mountain." When the pipers finished their lament, thirty Air Force F105s and twenty Navy F4s roared overhead, followed by low-flying Air Force One, which gently dipped its wings in final tribute. As the interment rites commenced, the caisson unit departed, plodding slowly along the serpentine roadways of the cemetery to the stables at Fort Myer.

The Kennedys and other mourners approach the gravesite in Arlington National Cemetery
The John F. Kennedy Library, Boston

The Kennedy family and other dignitaries at the interment service
The John F. Kennedy Library, Boston

At the conclusion of the religious ceremonies at the gravesite, the large Kennedy clan, surrounded by the host of other mourners, bowed their heads as Cardinal Cushing intoned the final words of the Roman Catholic committal service. Following that there was a twenty-one-gun salute, three volleys of musketry, and "Taps," played by an army bugler.

During the closing flag-folding ceremony, the Marine Band once again played John Kennedy's favorite navy hymn, whose rich chords resolve to the final phrase:

> Oh, hear us when we cry to thee
> For those in peril on the sea

After the body bearers folded the interment flag, the superintendent of Arlington National Cemetery presented it to Jackie, who then officially closed the burial service with Bobby Kennedy as they lit the eternal flame.

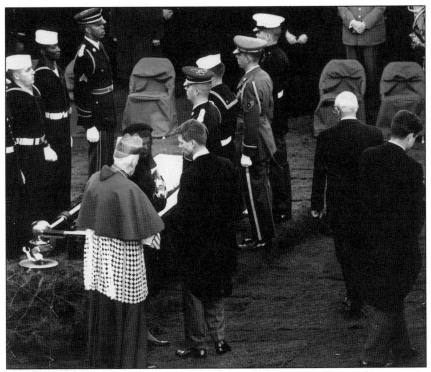

Richard Cardinal Cushing with Jacqueline and Bobby Kennedy at the conclusion of the interment service   *The John F. Kennedy Library, Boston*

As the crowd dispersed, and the dignitaries boarded their limousines to return to a reception at the White House, the caisson team and Black Jack, unharnessed and unsaddled, were being led to their stalls at the Fort Myer stables.

All of them had performed admirably under the most severe public scrutiny. Spectacular media coverage of John Kennedy's funeral conveyed dramatic images of the ceremonial horses to every corner of the world. But it was beautiful, spirited Black Jack who caught the people's fancy and became a celebrity.

From that time forward, admirers, especially children, would flock to see him at the stables where his popularity was enhanced by his engaging personality. Over a long and productive lifetime, he would amplify his renown, serving in the funerals of other presidents and in thousands of burials at Arlington National Cemetery.

The story of Black Jack's life and his rise to fame is fascinating. As it unfolds, you will discover how a fiery, unmanageable cavalry mount went on to become the most famous horse in the history of the U.S. Army.

CHAPTER TWO

Fort Reno, Oklahoma

FORT RENO was once an army garrison that encompassed 10,000 acres on the flat, rich grasslands of the southern Great Plains in central Oklahoma. Today Fort Reno is a sprawling complex of buildings and barns—many restored from the original military fort—that serves as an active research station operated by the U.S. Department of Agriculture. Having retained 6,700 acres of the old army post, it is ideally suited to the research its fifteen scientists and thirty support personnel conduct on forage and livestock production, weather, and the water cycle.

Although experimental herds of beef cattle and flocks of sheep now graze on the land where thousands of military horses and mules once roamed, the fort's present appearance is not substantially different from the bustling army outpost it once was.

The origin and development of the military fort was intricately related to the modern history of Oklahoma. And the history of Oklahoma, more than any other state in the union, is steeped in the lore of the American Indian. At one time, the land encompassing the present state of Oklahoma was known as Indian Territory. When its present name was chosen, it was derived from the combination of two Choctaw words: *okla*, meaning "people," and *humma*, meaning "red," literally denoting Oklahoma as "the land of the red people." No other name could be more appropriate for the state because Oklahoma was once a land inhabited by thirty-nine different Indian tribes, and is still the home of one-quarter of the entire native population of the United States.

Although this part of the nation is now tranquil and prosperous, it formerly was a region marred by conflict and battle. What's more, it was a territory that witnessed one of the darkest episodes ever perpetrated by the white man on the nation's aboriginal people.

Aerial view of Fort Reno, circa 1920   *El Reno Carnegie Library*

This shameful saga in American history was initiated in 1830 when the American Congress under President Andrew Jackson passed an act that forced the migration of many aboriginal tribes to this austere and undeveloped territory. By this cruel act of resettlement thousands of Cherokee, Creek, Choctaw, Chickasaw, and Seminole natives were evicted from their homes and farms and businesses and made to move westward into the eastern section of this unfamiliar, challenging environment. In the process, hundreds of native men, women and children died and were buried in unmarked graves along the route they called "The Trail of Tears."

As resentful as these civilized, resettled tribesmen could have been, it wasn't they who furiously fought the white man and forced the army to come in and build their forts. That lot fell to the Comanche, Kiowa, Apache, and others, including the nomadic Southern Cheyenne and Arapaho hunters who roamed the western part of the territory. These fearsome tribesmen, antagonized by the encroachment of white buffalo hunters and the incursion of other adventurers

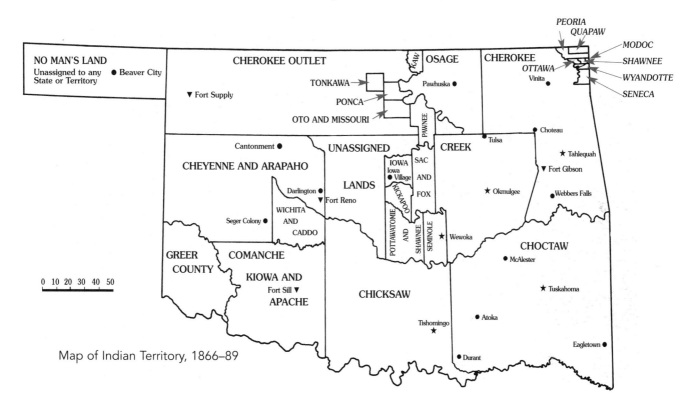

Map of Indian Territory, 1866–89

who threatened their way of life, attacked the intruders in their settlements or raided their westward wagon trains. Sometimes, usually with provocation, they vented their anger on the government-established Indian Agencies.

One of the outposts that came under threat of attack was the Darlington Indian Agency, which served the Cheyenne and Arapaho Indian Reservation on the banks of the North Canadian River about twenty-five miles west of the present site of Oklahoma City.

From time to time the turbulent western tribes, angered by being confined to their reservations, rose up in defiance. Such was the case in the last great Cheyenne Uprising of 1874. In response to this insurrection, the government sent in the army to protect the Darlington Agency and established Fort Reno on land adjacent to the Cheyenne–Arapaho reservation.

The first buildings of the new fort were erected between the years 1874 and 1876. It was during this time that the all-black "Buffalo Soldiers" of the 9th and 10th Cavalry and the 24th and 25th Infantry were assigned to the fort.

The Darlington Indian Agency, 1885

El Reno Carnegie Library

Cheyenne and Arapaho Indian scouts from Companies A and B at Fort Reno, circa 1880

Fort Reno Visitor Center, Canadian County Historical Society Collection

Enlisting Indian Scouts at Fort Reno, 1885   *El Reno Carnegie Library*

The Evans Brothers Post Trading Store at Fort Reno built in 1876   *El Reno Carnegie Library*

"Buffalo Soldiers" of the all-black 9th Cavalry at their camp on Long Island, New York in 1898 prior to their participation in the Spanish-American War *U.S. Army Military History Institute, Carlisle, Pennsylvania*

As well as an important post for keeping the natives in order, Fort Reno also served as a detention center for captured and surrendered Indians sent there from other northern forts. After the western tribes sued for peace and were confined on their reservations, there was little for the army to do at Fort Reno but patrol the region and demonstrate their presence.

Nevertheless, the fort continued to expand to a complex of some fifty buildings that included staff quarters, latrines, a guardhouse, maintenance and blacksmith shops, stables, oil houses, icehouses, a bakery and butcher shop, a sawmill, a bathhouse, a post office, and a hospital. The veterinary hospital on the base soon became one of the best of its kind in the United States.

Arapaho archers at Fort Reno, circa 1915

El Reno Carnegie Library

From 1880 to 1885, the garrison at Fort Reno was primarily preoccupied with the incursions of renegade white settlers. In 1885, Gen. Philip H. Sheridan of Civil War fame arrived at the fort and recommended to President Grover Cleveland that all non-Indian leases be terminated in Indian Territory and that unauthorized persons be removed from Indian land.

When the infamous Boomers attempted to promote occupation of the fertile unassigned lands of the Indian Territory before they were legally open to white settlement, the army evicted them and imprisoned their leader and several of his henchmen in the fort's stockade.

Later, in 1889, when portions of the Indian Territory were about to be opened for authorized settlement, it was the soldiers from Fort Reno who guarded the boundaries and kept order among the throngs of people who camped along the border waiting for the signal to stake a land claim in the territory. It was the Fort Reno troops who prevented the Sooners—another group attempting to jump the gun—from encroaching on the land before the appointed time and who, at noon on April 22, 1889, fired the shots to signal the start of the great race for property in the territory.

With the opening of the land to settlement and the rapid growth and domination of the white people in the territory, there was soon no further need of a military force in the area and the fort gradually fell into disuse. It was abandoned as an army post in 1908.

That same year Fort Reno was taken over by the U.S. Quartermaster Department, whose function since the days of the American Revolution was the procurement and training of animals for military use. The Quartermaster Corps immediately re-established the fort as the country's first army remount depot.

The function of the Remount Service was to procure, process, train, and issue horses, mules and dogs for the army. The Service also conditioned the horses and provided initial rider training for new cavalry recruits.

One of their first major tasks was to fence the perimeter of the entire fort and cross-fence the pasture fields, a chore that took almost three years to complete. During this time the Service also began seeding the land for forage crops, gradually expanding this enterprise until 1,800 acres were under cultivation.

Meanwhile, expert staff at the fort took over the responsibility of supervising the horse-breeding program, which was designed to improve the quality of army horses. Previously, army horses and mules had been purchased from breeders under contract, but the practice had proven unsatisfactory.

When the U.S. entered World War I, Fort Reno became a very active garrison. The Remount Service was required to supply the enormous number of replacement riding horses and draft animals that were needed to haul ammunition, water, food, heavy artillery, and the wagons

Constructing one of the Fort Reno stables, circa 1910   *Fort Reno Visitor Center Collection*

required to evacuate the wounded. During the war, Fort Reno played a major role in helping supply the total of 571,000 horses and mules that were processed through the entire remount system. At that time the number of remount stations was massive. Even when the war ended, the Quartermaster Corps still maintained thirty-nine remount depots across the U.S. with a capacity of over 200,000 animals.

U.S. Cavalry drill charge, Fort Reno, 1918 *U.S. Army Military History Institute, Carlisle, Pennsylvania*

U.S. Cavalry training near Fort Reno, circa 1920
Fort Reno Visitor Center, Canadian County Historical Society Collection

U.S. engineers with
pack mules and
horses passing
through Romagne-
sous-Montfaucon,
France, on their way
to the front,
November 1918
*U.S. Army Military
History Institute,
Carlisle, Pennsylvania*

By 1925 Fort Reno had developed into a major outpost with a military staff of 115 men supported by a complement of fifty civilians. There were 110 buildings on site and stables that housed 800 horses. A racetrack and polo field were developed at the fort and 100 polo ponies were boarded and conditioned there to maintain a crack polo team on the base. The fort's polo program was so advanced that the national polo meet was hosted there in 1925. This elaborate event drew teams from across the country that were fêted at gala dinners and formal dances. These occasions, in turn, spawned other elegant social functions.

Two thousand horses were trained and shipped from Fort Reno in 1927. Motorization and mechanization in the military reduced the need for animals in the 1930s, but did not make them completely obsolete. In order to perpetuate good cavalry stock, civilian breeding farms were maintained under contract and the army's horse-breeding program resumed.

By 1940 horses and mules had been replaced by motor transport in most military units, but the army still maintained two cavalry divisions with a total of 16,800 horses under saddle and

Automobiles parked near the polo grounds at Fort Reno, circa 1920   *El Reno Carnegie Library*

harness. Fort Reno continued to serve as a remount depot to ensure that these horses were trained and conditioned and to teach the horsemen and teamsters how to handle, ride or drive them.

By 1943, with the increased use of trucks and Jeeps, there was little demand for horses overseas. However, the coast guard required 3,000 horses to patrol American beaches in order to sound the alert against enemy submarines.

In 1944, the eastern portion of Fort Reno served as an internment camp for 1,000 German prisoners of war taken captive in North Africa. These captured soldiers, most of whom were members of Gen. Erwin Rommel's Afrika Corps, worked as laborers at the remount station and helped build a new fort chapel. They also were loaned out to work on local farms.

Through 1945, 14,000 mules were procured and trained at the remount depots to be sent overseas where they were employed to negotiate the rugged jungle or mountain terrain in Tunisia, Burma, and northern Italy.

Even after the war's end, Fort Reno continued a diminished program of training horses and riders. Cavalry staff at the fort continued to purchase stallions for breeding purposes and to select and inspect civilian horse-breeding centers. But the primary focus at this time for the Remount Branch across the country was on the disposal of cavalry horses rather than on their procurement.

Fort Reno Officers' Club and the race track, 1945

El Reno Carnegie Library

As a result many fine animals were sold off to foreign countries that still maintained mounted units for cavalry, police or ceremonial duties. During one three-day auction at Fort Reno, 3,000 horses were sold on the block.

The only horses retained by the U.S. government were those deemed suitable for ceremonial purposes at Arlington National Cemetery. Because these horses performed sensitive, high-profile duties at the graveyard, their appearance had to meet very rigid standards assuring that their conformation, size, and color were exactly right.

Photos showing the last U.S. horse-
drawn artillery unit before its final
march from Fort Sill, Oklahoma, to
Fort Reno, 1940
El Reno Carnegie Library

Above: German prisoners of war at Fort Reno, 1944
Fort Reno Visitor Center, Robert Awald Collection

Right: Fort Reno chapel built by German prisoners of war, 1945 *Fort Reno Visitor Center*

It was in 1947 during this time of cavalry dispersal that Black Jack was born on one of the breeding farms near Arkansas City, Kansas, a small community located a few miles above the northern boundary of Oklahoma. Being an elegant combination of Morgan and quarter horse, he was an attractive and sturdy foal that showed lots of promise. In retrospect, many people believe that his date of birth seemed to destine him for distinction. He was foaled on January 19, the same birth date as that of legendary Confederate general Robert E. Lee.

Furthermore, the name he was given offered portents of greatness. Being a handsome, jet-black foal with only a small, white star on his forehead, he was named after Gen. John J. "Black

Jack" Pershing, whose reputation was revered in Oklahoma. It was Pershing who first rode to national prominence as the commander of twelve thousand regulars of the First Oklahoma Regiment that went deep into Mexico in pursuit of Pancho Villa in 1916.

Gen. Robert E. Lee (1807–70) on Traveller   *U.S. Army Military History Institute, Carlisle, Pennsylvania*

Gen. John J. Pershing leading his cavalry troops across the Rio Grande in 1916
U.S. Army Military History Institute, Carlisle, Pennsylvania

Not long after that Pershing became supreme commander of the American Expeditionary Force, leading his doughboys to victory in Europe during World War I. So distinguished were Pershing's military exploits that he retains the honor of being one of only two U.S. officers awarded the exalted rank of General of the Armies. The only other American to achieve such august status is the country's first president, General of the Armies George Washington.

At the time of Black Jack's birth, Pershing was still a cherished memory in Oklahoma, an honorable old soldier fading away in the twilight of his life. Sixteen months later Pershing died and was buried in Arlington National Cemetery.

When Black Jack was three years old, he was purchased from the breeding farm by a horse dealer named Babe Jones, who had started his career giving "wind tests" to horses and selling those that passed the trials to the army during World War I. He also helped the army set up their cooperative breeding program where quality stallions were loaned to ranchers throughout the region.

Although Babe Jones liked the look of Black Jack, he didn't judge him to be exceptional. To Jones, Black Jack was just another stock horse that might develop into a reasonably good cavalry mount. The buyers at Fort Reno agreed with his assessment and purchased Black Jack for a new U.S. foreign aid program that would ultimately process thousands of mules and horses for shipment overseas. Like all the other animals acquired for the program, Black Jack was hauled to Fort Reno where he was branded, groomed, and inoculated for eventual shipment to either Greece or Turkey.

Upon arriving at the fort, Black Jack was marked with the "US" brand on his left shoulder and the army serial number 2V56 on the left side of his neck. These identification markings proved to be another distinction that set Black Jack apart because he was the last Quartermaster-issued horse branded by the U.S. Army.

Black Jack's transfer to Fort Reno must have been a big adjustment for him. Except for the flat plains that stretched out for miles in every direction, the physical appearance of his new home was entirely different. The friendly confines of his old corral and stable were replaced by huge barns and sheds and a myriad of unfamiliar buildings of every shape and size. The care he received was equally good, but instead of the few familiar faces that used to dote on him, the fort was bustling with uniformed strangers and civilian stable hands who went about their chores with a detached, businesslike approach. No longer were there just a few mares and yearlings to keep him company, but hundreds of horses of every color sharing the corrals and pastures and stables.

And the horses arrived and departed on a regular basis. As soon as they were broken and trained, they were on their way. At the peak of its operation, Fort Reno shipped out 800 horses every forty-five days. That number was reduced considerably by the time Black Jack arrived and slowed to a trickle by the time he left. In the interim, like every other horse at the depot, Black Jack had to endure the rigors of training.

It was not a process he relished. The horses at the fort were broken by the stable hands, most of whom came from El Reno, a city of 16,000 seven miles away. Because the work was so rugged and physically demanding, the trainers were a tough bunch of horsemen who broke and trained the animals with a firm and unrelenting approach.

Right from the start, Black Jack made it clear that he did not like the saddle and hated being ridden. When mounted he became unruly and with his indomitable spirit threw rider after rider, leaving them sitting in the dust while he bucked riotously around the training corral.

Gradually the riders got him under a semblance of control but he never completely lost his fractious, unpredictable edge. All the trainers at the fort knew his reputation and handled him with caution.

At the same time, everyone admired his beautiful looks. He had a marvelous head, a wide, handsome face, sound legs and a muscular body that rippled with definition. At maturity he stood 15.1 hands and weighed almost 1,200 pounds, which he carried with an air of authority.

His physical appearance combined with his fervid temperament made him a favorite at the fort. While the administration shipped out one horse after another, they were reluctant to sell Black Jack as a common stock horse and sought a special placement for him.

Fate intervened when the army advised they were looking for a smart, attractive horse to serve on the Caisson Platoon at Fort Myer, Virginia, across the Potomac River from Washington, D.C.

After some consultation between the principals at both forts, a transfer was arranged and Black Jack was loaded aboard a cattle car destined for Virginia.

There were few at Fort Reno who gave much thought to Black Jack's departure. He was just another good-looking horse, albeit a difficult one, who had come and gone. At Fort Myer there were others who awaited his arrival with much the same attitude.

Certainly no one at either fort or anywhere in between had the faintest idea of how much this cantankerous black gelding would eventually contribute to the glory of the American army and the honor of the nation.

CHAPTER THREE

Fort Myer, Virginia

BLACK JACK'S long and tedious train ride from Oklahoma to Fort Myer transported him from a massive, open, western-style ranch complex to a smaller, more compact post that in many ways resembles a well-developed, turn-of-the-century, middle-class American town.

An aerial view of a section of Fort Myer showing Summerall Field, the Headquarters Building (center), Brucker Hall, the home of the U.S. Army Band (right), and the steeple of the Old Post Chapel in the distance

Tom Mani, Military District of Washington Public Affairs Office

Fort Myer Headquarters on Lee Avenue
Andy Garlatti, Windsor, Ontario

Officers' homes on Lee Avenue, Fort Myer
Ray Kosi, Newport Beach, California

A number of the attractive residences on the post have housed famous officers and their families. On the hillside of the fort that offers a distant but clear view of Washington is a residence called "Quarters One," the designated home of the army chief of staff. Over the years it has been the family residence of such luminaries as Generals Douglas MacArthur, George Marshall, Dwight D. Eisenhower and Omar Bradley.

General of the Army
Douglas MacArthur
(1880–1964)
*The MacArthur Memorial
Library and Archives,
Norfolk, Virginia*

Gen. George Marshall
(1880–1959)
*U.S. Army Military History
Institute, Carlisle,
Pennsylvania*

Gen. Dwight D. Eisenhower
(1890–1969), thirty-fourth
president of the United States
*U.S. Army Military History
Institute, Carlisle,
Pennsylvania*

Gen. Omar Bradley
(1893–1981)
*U.S. Army Military History
Institute, Carlisle,
Pennsylvania*

"Quarters Six" is the official residence of the Chairman of the Joint Chiefs of Staff. One of its more recent distinguished occupants was Gen. Colin Powell, who went on to become U.S. secretary of state.

"Quarters Seven," which originally had twenty-six rooms, is the home of the chief of staff of the air force.

Twenty-six of the pleasant, red-brick residences on the post are now assigned to high-ranking officers and their families, many on a street known as "Generals Row." The standing joke is that there are more generals at Fort Myer than there are soldiers.

Since Fort Myer's inception, it has known a long and distinguished line of commanding officers. The most famous of these were Gen. George S. Patton Jr. (1938) who led his troops to

Gen. Colin Powell (1937-)
U.S. Army Military History Institute, Carlisle, Pennsylvania

Gen. George Patton (1885–1945)
U.S. Army Military History Institute, Carlisle, Pennsylvania

Gen. Jonathan Wainwright (1883–1953)
U.S. Army Military History Institute, Carlisle, Pennsylvania

Summerall Field, Fort Myer, Virginia

Andy Garlatti, Windsor, Ontario

victory in Morocco, Sicily, and France in World War II, and Gen. Jonathan Wainwright (1936), who valiantly fought the Japanese at the Corregidor Island fortress off the Bataan peninsula.

The majority of the facilities on the post have been built around Summerall Field, a mammoth, sodded parade ground that is equal in area to four football fields laid end to end.

Not far from one corner of the parade field are the stables that house the horses of the only official missioned unit still maintained by the Department of Defense. The two stables now in use are a far cry from the vast number employed during the glory days of the U.S. Cavalry prior to World War I. Back then, Fort Myer had row on row of operational stables that were essential to

Twelve-horse unit of The Old Guard parading at a change-of-command ceremony on Summerall Field, Fort Myer
Jim Friedman, Bedford Heights, Ohio

The Caisson Platoon stables at
Fort Myer, 2000
*Ray Kosi, Newport Beach,
California*

Interior of the Fort Myer stables
Andy Garlatti, Windsor, Ontario

accommodate over a thousand horses. Many of those barns have long since been converted to facilities now used for other purposes.

When Black Jack arrived in 1952, the stable still in operation provided stalls for some twenty-six horses. Its primary function was to house the horses used for the ceremonial funerals that take place daily in Arlington National Cemetery, only a half mile away.

Many of the funeral processions at the cemetery commence at The Old Post Chapel, located adjacent to Chapel Gate at the rear of the cemetery. This quaint, colonial-style chapel was completed in 1935 under the direction of then Maj. George S. Patton, Jr.

Although most of the buildings in the fort were erected at the turn of the twentieth century, Fort Myer's history goes back well beyond that.

The first military post established in the vicinity of Fort Myer was a line of earthen works raised on the banks of the Potomac River to protect Washington from attack by the British in the War of 1812.

At one time the land currently occupied by Fort Myer belonged to George Washington Parke Custis, the grandson of Martha Washington, who owned the land where the fort and Arlington National Cemetery now stand. Custis's daughter married a young army lieutenant, Robert E. Lee, who saved the extensive estate from bankruptcy in 1858, only to lose it during the Civil War.

The Custis-Lee mansion in Arlington National Cemetery
The Military District of Washington

At the onset of that war, Lee was offered command of the Union Army, but declined and left the estate in 1861 to lead the Confederate Army of Virginia. He never returned to the mansion. Within a few months of Lee's departure, the property was confiscated by the Union for military purposes. Three years later it was bought at auction by the U.S. government because the Lees were unable to comply with a newly passed law that required them to appear in person to pay their land taxes.

Gen. Robert E. Lee (1807–70)
U.S. Army Military History Institute, Carlisle, Pennsylvania

After the government purchased the property, it designated part of the grounds of the Custis-Lee estate to be used as a national burial ground for war dead. The remainder of the land became Fort Whipple, whose location on the bluffs overlooking the Potomac River was considered the most strategic point to defend the Union capital. When the Civil War ended, the Signal Corps took over the army post because the post's elevation offered an ideal location for visual communications.

In 1881, to eliminate confusion with another Fort Whipple in Arizona, the Virginia post was renamed Fort Myer. The Signal Corps manned the post until 1887, when Gen. Philip H. Sheridan, the U.S. Army's commanding general, decided to convert the post into the cavalry showplace of the nation. The communications unit was transferred out and horsemen were assigned to the fort. As a result, lengthy rows of stables were constructed to house the 1,500 horses procured for the riders. For the next twenty-two years, army horsemanship at Fort Myer became an important part of the military and social life of Washington.

Horsemanship was not the only focus of the post. In 1908, Orville Wright made the first-ever military test flight from the fort's present-day parade grounds and managed to keep his plane aloft for one minute and eleven seconds. The second test flight stayed up for four minutes but ended in a tragic crash severely injuring Wright and killing his passenger, Lt. Thomas Selfridge.

The sound of music also fills the air in the fort. In 1942, the U.S. Army Band "Pershing's Own" was moved to Fort Myer. In 1960, a sixty-nine-member fife and drum corps made the fort its permanent home. Dressed in tricorn hats, wigs, and colonial musicians' uniforms, they march and perform at ceremonial functions rekindling the "Spirit of '76."

In 1948 two battalions of the 3rd U.S. Infantry Regiment, the oldest regular U.S. Army regiment, were reactivated and assigned to Fort Myer. This unit, first mustered in 1784 in the time of George Washington and thus known as "The Old Guard," assumed responsibility for the army's ceremonial and security duties in Washington D.C.

The Old Guard Fife and Drum Corps
Peter Fillman, Toronto, Ontario

Ever since then they have served as the official honor guard and escort for the president and are required to conduct military ceremonies at the White House, the Pentagon, and national memorials within the Military District of Washington. The Old Guard is also responsible for maintaining a twenty-four hour vigil at the Tomb of the Unknowns in Arlington National Cemetery.

One of The Old Guard's most honorable duties was delegated to their Caisson Platoon, which is required to provide mounted military funeral escorts at Arlington National Cemetery and to participate in the state funerals of high-ranking government officials. This is a most demanding responsibility because sometimes the funerals exceed more than eight in a day.

It was to this Old Guard Caisson Platoon that Black Jack was assigned. When he arrived at the stables on November 22, 1952, Black Jack was quarantined for twenty-one days in a stall inside the indoor riding arena to make sure he was sound and healthy and to protect the other horses from any illness he might have contracted en route.

Before being shipped to the caisson unit, all horses were supposed to be broken to ride, but they were not always ready for the harness. Consequently, after Black Jack's release from

Horses and riders training at Fort Myer, 2000
Charles Hickey, Essex, Ontario

quarantine, he was processed through a nine-day trial of harness testing. Although this did not go entirely smoothly, he passed his tests and then went into basic training.

Every step of the way, Black Jack was under the scrutiny of the platoon leader. Although he and everyone else in the platoon, from the riders to the farrier to the leather smith, were impressed with Black Jack's beauty and faultless conformation, they were also soon made aware of Black Jack's spirited temperament. Consequently they knew that training him for the disciplined duties he would be required to perform would present a considerable challenge.

First Black Jack had to be trained to the harness so that he could work with the other horses pulling the caisson. These antiquated wagons, used by the U.S. Army since the 1800s, were redesigned in 1918 to carry ammunition chests, spare wheels and gunnery tools. Later, when the caissons became obsolete, they were modified for funeral purposes and fitted with a flat platform suitable for bearing a coffin.

At Fort Myer, the caisson is pulled by three pairs of matched horses, either all black or all gray in color. The pair closest to the wagon does most of the actual pulling and is called the wheel pair.

The Old Guard grays getting ready for duty at Fort Myer
Charles Hickey, Essex, Ontario

45

Normally they are the biggest of the three pairs of horses, some standing sixteen hands tall (a hand equals four inches) at the shoulder and weighing up to 1,400 pounds.

Ahead of the wheel pair is the swing pair, comprised of horses that need not be quite so big or strong. The swing pair follows the lead pair, which guides the direction of the caisson and sets the pace. These lead horses can be the smallest of the six but must be intelligent and reliable in the performance of their duties.

Many of the caisson horses, especially the wheel pairs, are a breed known as a "draft-cross," which was originally developed to work in the fields. Their bloodlines come from a mixture of Percheron and Thoroughbred stock, or Percheron and Morgan, or a combination of Percheron and quarter horse. The Percheron influence gives them their size, a good foot that holds up on hard surfaces, and a quiet disposition. The genetics from the smaller type horses contribute to their mobility and endurance.

A caisson unit leaving the stables at Fort Myer
Charles Hickey, Essex, Ontario

The Old Guard riders in training at Fort Myer
Charles Hickey, Essex, Ontario

The final result is a mobile horse that requires low maintenance and does not break down under daily use in harness.

Black Jack's breeding made him somewhat smaller and lighter than many of the horses in the stables. At 15.1 hands and 1,126 pounds, his size was best suited for the lead pair. Nevertheless, he still had to take his turn training in all positions of the team.

All of the pulling horses of the caisson unit are saddled but only those on the left are ridden. Traditionally the horses on the right had no riders because they were expected to carry feed and provisions on their backs. However, whether the harnessed horses work on the left or right side, all of them must be trained to carry a rider.

Unfortunately, no matter at which position they tried Black Jack, he did not take well to the training. He didn't like being harnessed, was irritable when confined to the traces, and became agitated when connected to the other horses. On the march, he wasn't wild or unmanageable but seemed to have an independent air that made him unhappy and reluctant to cooperate. It was obvious to the trainers that being part of a team was not something he enjoyed.

A section sergeant ready for duty at Fort Myer
Peter Fillman, Toronto, Ontario

Caparisoned horse and walker returning from a funeral in Arlington National Cemetery, 2000
Peter Fillman, Toronto, Ontario

So they tried him as the section horse, which is ridden on the left side of the three pulling pairs by the section sergeant in charge of the ceremonial entourage. Black Jack quickly made it obvious that he was ill suited for this assignment, too, because he clearly disliked being ridden. All of the riders in the platoon who mounted him for training soon learned they had to be extremely careful how they handled him.

Because the riders who worked with Black Jack found him unpredictable, the platoon leader was concerned. He realized it could prove to be embarrassing if Black Jack became difficult while participating in the solemnity of a funeral cortege.

Any other horse exhibiting such unsatisfactory tendencies would have been immediately released from the Caisson Platoon. But Black Jack was so sleek and beautiful, the platoon leader was reluctant to let him go.

Finally he came to the conclusion that there was only one other assignment with the Caisson Platoon that Black Jack might be able to fulfill—the role of the caparisoned horse.

"Caparison" is an obscure and antiquated term that is derived from the French word for "cape." In more recent times it refers to the ornamental covering on a ceremonial horse, most often one that is participating in a funeral. At Fort Myer the term pertained to the riderless horse that follows the caisson in funerals for civilian dignitaries, officers of the military with rider service in their background, and army and marine corps officers above the rank of colonel.

Based on tradition, the fort's riderless horse was saddled, adorned with a saber, and had spurred cavalry boots placed in reverse position in the stirrups. Custom also dictated that the caparisoned horse be black and dramatically striking in appearance.

The tradition of the riderless horse dates back to the time of the early Saxons. It was also a custom utilized by the Tartars to honor their fearless leaders such as Genghis Khan and Tamerlane. From that long-ago era, continuing up to the eighteenth century, the chargers of great military commanders were hooded, sacrificed, and buried with their masters so they could serve them in the afterworld. Some western American Indians followed a similar ritual. In 1838, Blackhawk, a chief of the Omahas, was reportedly buried sitting on his horse.

In more modern times, because it became unacceptable to kill and bury horses with their riders, a military tradition evolved whereby the fallen hero's horse followed him in his funeral procession. The boots reversed in the stirrups of the saddle signified the fact that the horse's master would never ride again and that as commander he was looking back at his troops one last time.

One of the earliest uses of the riderless horse in presidential history occurred in the Mount Vernon cortege for Gen. George Washington. His horse carried his saddle, holster, and pistols in the procession. At the 1919 funeral of Gen. George Bell at Arlington National Cemetery, the caparisoned horse wore a full-length black "housing" or covering cloth. In more recent times, a

Official White House portrait of George Washington (1732–99), first president of the United States

Official White House portrait of Franklin Delano Roosevelt (1882–1945) thirty-second president of the United States

similar full-length housing was worn by the riderless horse in the funeral ceremony for Franklin Delano Roosevelt at Hyde Park, New York, in 1945.

Prior to Roosevelt's funeral, when Gen. "Black Jack" Pershing became seriously ill and there was little hope of his surviving, his two favorite horses, Jeff and Kidron, were brought to Fort Myer with the expectation that they would be used in his funeral cortege. However, the resilient old general recovered and ironically outlived both of his horses.

So it was that the time-honored custom of the riderless horse was very much in practice when Black Jack arrived at Fort Myer. And the Caisson Platoon leader, considering Black Jack's beauty and his reluctance to be ridden, decided to give him a try at this distinguished assignment. His only concern was whether or not Black Jack's fiery temperament would make him difficult to handle and detract from the dignity of the funeral cortege.

The platoon leader decided there was only one way to find out. When the weather warmed and the road conditions were favorable, he assigned Black Jack as the caparisoned horse for a funeral in Arlington National Cemetery. And he almost came to regret his decision.

While waiting outside The Old Post Chapel for the casket to emerge, Black Jack was restless, requiring constant attention by his handler. When the cortege got rolling and made its way through the cemetery, Black Jack repeatedly tugged his head up and down and pranced about frenetically, appearing almost out of control. Unfortunately, his antics were in full view of the mourners who walked immediately behind him.

During the interment ceremony he continued his unsettled behavior on the roadway as his companion horses stood calm and patient in their traces. Even after the gun volley was fired at the grave and the ceremonies were concluded, Black Jack continued his animated conduct all the way back to the stables.

The platoon leader had made it a point to observe Black Jack's performance that day and, when the funeral was ended, went to the family of the deceased to apologize for Black Jack's skittish behavior. To his surprise, they not only took no offense at Black Jack's conduct, they *liked* the way he had behaved. They felt that his fiery spirit was most appropriate because it reminded them of the energy and enthusiasm of their departed relative. Several in the family expressed appreciation for Black Jack's vital contribution to the otherwise sorrowful event.

Their positive comments were enlightening to the platoon leader and made him feel more comfortable using Black Jack in other funeral processions. Whenever he did, just as before, the family's response to Black Jack's performance was enthusiastic. It soon became apparent that Black Jack's beauty and vitality were a captivating combination that they admired.

What's more, Black Jack seemed to thrive on the attention he attracted. It was as if he knew he was important and relished the admiration he received.

His lively personality also made him a favorite in the barn. Seldom did a soldier pass

Black Jack and his walker in Arlington National Cemetery, 1954
The U.S. Army and The Old Guard Museum, Fort Myer, Virginia

his stall without stopping to rub his nose and offer a friendly greeting. When visitors came to the stables, they admired all the horses in the stables but appeared to be magnetically drawn to Black Jack.

The big grays like Prince from Kansas and Cloud Burst from Missouri were bigger, each weighing over 1,300 pounds. Blue from Oklahoma and Capp from Texas were more stately. Blue

Black Jack with his walker, Corporal Paul Minugh, 1957

The U.S. Army and The Old Guard Museum, Fort Myer, Virginia

Dare was a smart and pleasant lead horse from Fort Worth. Rocket and Pretty Boy, both from Fort Reno, were as attractive and friendly as Black Jack. The huge blacks like Big Max, Prospect, and Zipper were equally impressive.

But invariably it was Black Jack's elegance and his enthusiasm that made him the people's choice. Almost every person who came to visit the barn stopped to pet him. Some fed him sugar cubes or gingerly offered him an apple. Often Black Jack responded by showing his teeth as if he were smiling in delight.

Nevertheless, as popular as Black Jack was in the stables, it was his work in the cemetery as the caparisoned horse that would ultimately lead him to fame. Each trip he made served as a preliminary to his destiny as, time after time in his irrepressible manner, he followed the flag-draped caisson along the labyrinthine roadways of Arlington National Cemetery.

The U.S. Army Band, "Pershing's Own," stationed at Fort Myer, Virginia since 1942   *The U.S. Army Band*

CHAPTER FOUR

Arlington National Cemetery

Arlington National Cemetery with Arlington House on the hill in the distance

Warren G. Miller, Kensington, Maryland

TO UNDERSTAND the significance of Black Jack's responsibilities with the Caisson Platoon, one must comprehend the patriotic grandeur of Arlington National Cemetery. It is one of the rare places in America where the beauty of its landscape and the symbolism of its endless monuments combine in such a spectacular fashion. Here, the rolling hills and winding roads lined with rich foliage provide a perfect setting for the final resting place of hundreds of thousands of brave men and women who have faithfully served their country.

The poignant splendor of Arlington National Cemetery
Warren G. Miller, Kensington, Maryland

These gardens of stone are spread across vast manicured lawns marking row after measured row of honored plots in a shrine that once was the farmland of Robert E. Lee. Beneath the headstones lie the remains of servicemen and women who have served in every war the United States has ever fought. The names inscribed on the stones are a veritable roll call of the military history of the nation, ranging from common soldiers of the American Revolution to the most august generals who ever led U.S. troops into battle.

Prior to the onset of the Civil War in 1861, Robert E. Lee and his family vacated their Virginia property, and shortly thereafter the federal government established the Custis-Lee mansion, known as Arlington House, as their headquarters for the defense

Row on row of graves at Arlington National Cemetery
Andy Garlatti, Windsor, Ontario

of Washington. From that time until 1864, the large number of Union troops stationed there transformed the rustic estate into a bustling military encampment.

During the early years of the Civil War, much of the fighting took place on battlefields not far from Washington. Consequently, hordes of wounded soldiers were sent to hospitals there, and many died. To accommodate their burials, in 1862 military cemeteries were established in Alexandria, Virginia, and Washington. They were soon filled nearly to capacity.

As the war progressed and Union fatalities continued to mount, burial space became more and more scarce. Still, little thought was given to using the Lee estate as a burial ground. In part this was due to the fact that in 1863 the federal government established a model community on the property for fugitive or liberated slaves. Called Freedman's Village, the settlement was a place where more than 1,100 ex-slaves were given land on which to farm and live. Houses were erected and a hospital, a church, a home for the aged and disabled, and a large industrial school were built to serve the inhabitants.

By 1864, the need for burial space in Washington had become critical. Abraham Lincoln's secretary of war, Edwin M. Stanton, ordered the quartermaster general, Brig. Gen. Montgomery Meigs, a talented engineer and an accomplished architect, to do a survey and suggest a new site for a military graveyard. Meigs did not do a survey, but it didn't take him long to make his recommendation.

Meigs knew—and at one time admired—Robert E. Lee, having worked with him in 1837 on

A piper at the tomb of Brig. Gen. Montgomery Meigs
Warren G. Miller, Kensington, Maryland

a navigational engineering assignment on the Mississippi River near St. Louis. But the Civil War changed Meigs's attitude towards Lee. As an ardent patriot, Meigs considered those fighting for the Southern cause to be traitors; and he formed the same contemptible opinion of Lee. Being an egotistical man with a violent temper, Meigs immediately ordered that the new military cemetery should be located on the grounds of Robert E. Lee's Arlington estate.

Secretary of War Stanton agreed, and on June 15, 1864, during the time the ex-slaves were living in Freedman's Village, he officially designated Arlington House and 200 acres of its adjoining grounds as a military cemetery.

Since then, the remains of more than 275,000 people have been buried on the grounds. Presently, the annual number of funerals exceeds 5,400 per year. In addition to the in-ground burials, the cemetery has a columbarium with 50,000 niches for cremated remains. There are plans in progress to expand that capacity three times over.

When Arlington National Cemetery first opened in 1864, it was, of course, intended for use as a graveyard for Union soldiers killed in the Civil War. On Montgomery Meigs's orders the first soldiers interred there were to be buried close by Robert E. Lee's former mansion, where he had lived only three years previously. When Meigs discovered that these first bodies were buried one quarter of a mile away from the house, he had twenty-six more corpses delivered to the grounds and personally supervised their interment in rows adjacent to Arlington House. Other Union fatalities were interred in Mrs. Lee's cherished rose garden. The placement of these graves was clearly motivated by Meigs's hatred of Lee and his desire to retaliate against the wily Confederate general whom he considered to be a turncoat.

Two unknown Union soldiers were laid to rest in Arlington National Cemetery in 1864, making them the first of nearly 5,000 unknowns now buried in the cemetery. Some 1,500 United States colored troops of the Civil War were also buried in the cemetery, the first black American combat soldiers to die for their country.

In Section 27 of the graveyard lie more than 3,800 former slaves, who were called "contrabands" during the Civil War. Their markers are designated with either the word "Civilian" or "Citizen."

Long after the Civil War ended, Union Gen. Philip H. Sheridan was buried on the front lawn of the mansion. His tombstone, tinged with moss-green markings, stands

Graves of Union soldiers buried beside Arlington House on the direct orders of Montgomery Meigs
Warren G. Miller, Kensington, Maryland

Headstones of former slaves buried in Section 27
Warren G. Miller, Kensington, Maryland

dramatically alone on top of the steep hill that runs down to the Potomac.

As time passed, public support for the ex-slaves in Freedman's Village gradually declined and fewer resources were provided for the residents. There was also an ever-increasing need for the burial land they occupied in the cemetery. Finally, because the village was located on a military reservation, federal law prohibited the inhabitants from residing there, and they were turned out in 1890 with only ninety days' notice. Only the graves of their dead remain to mark the site of their settlement.

Gen. Philip H. Sheridan
(1831–88)
*U.S. Army Military
History Institute,
Carlisle, Pennsylvania*

Gen. Sheridan's
headstone on the
lawn in front of
Arlington House
*Warren G. Miller,
Kensington, Maryland*

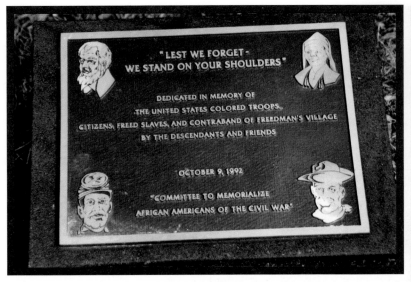

Plaque in Arlington National Cemetery honoring U.S. colored troops and the deceased of Freedman's Village (above)
Warren G. Miller, Kensington, Maryland

The headstone on the grave of Pvt. Christman, the first serviceman to be buried in Arlington National Cemetery (right)
Warren G. Miller, Kensington, Maryland

Since then, eligibility rules for burial in the cemetery have evolved. These pertain to active, retired, and certain decorated U.S. military personnel as well as distinguished civilians with military service in their backgrounds. Moreover, each person deemed eligible for burial in the cemetery is also allowed to have two family members (his/her spouse and one unmarried child) buried there. As a consequence, there was concern that the graveyard would be filled to capacity by the year 2005. However, the cemetery recently finalized the purchase of another sixty acres, which will greatly extend that timeline.

Currently, 4.5 million visitors per year come to Arlington National Cemetery to pay their respects to a fallen friend or relative or to visit the Kennedy gravesite. As they wend their way through the grounds, they are surrounded by the stone archives of the nation. These range from the tombstone of Pvt. William Henry Christman, the first serviceman buried in the cemetery, to more recent markers such as that of Maj. Marie Therese Rossi, a U.S. Army helicopter pilot killed the day after the cease-fire that ended operation Desert Storm.

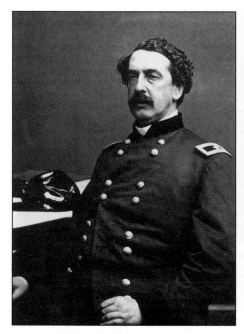

Brevet General Abner
Doubleday (1819–93)
*U.S. Army Military History
Institute, Carlisle,
Pennsylvania*

Brevet General Abner
Doubleday's tombstone in
Arlington National Cemetery
*Warren G. Miller,
Kensington, Maryland*

Other names etched in the stones provide a lengthy roster of well-known citizens, many of them American heroes. An abbreviated list of these patriots includes:

Brevet Brig. Gen. Abner Doubleday, Civil War; baseball innovator who codified rules of baseball

Maj. Gen. Philip Kearney, Civil War

Gen. Claire Chennault, U.S. Air Force Flying Tigers, WW II

LTC Frederick Benteen, with Custer at the Little Big Horn

Col. William Jennings Bryan, secretary of state; presidential candidate

Sgt. Joe "Louis" Barrow, heavyweight boxing champion of the world

Staff Sgt. Frank Reynolds, ABC news anchorman

Rear Adm. Robert Peary, first to reach the North Pole

Medgar Evers, Mississippi civil rights activist

Lt. James Forrestal, first secretary of defense, WW II

General of the Armies John J.
"Black Jack" Pershing
(1860–1948)
*U.S. Army Military History
Institute, Carlisle, Pennsylvania*

Gen. Pershing insisted on a
modest headstone similar to
those used for the troops who
fought under his command. The
distinction of his grave is marked
by its solitary position in the
graveyard.
*Warren G. Miller, Kensington,
Maryland*

Three of the six marines who raised the flag on Iwo
    Jima in WW II: Sgt. Michael Strank, Pfc. Rene
    Gagnon, and Pima native American Pfc. Ira Hayes
Gen. John J. Pershing, General of the Armies, WW I
Adm. Richard Byrd, Arctic explorer
Dr. Anita Newcomb Magee, founder of the Army
    Nursing Corps in 1900
Maj. Audie Murphy, most decorated U.S. soldier of
    WW II
Adm. Hyman Rickover, father of the U.S. nuclear
    navy
Maj. Walter Reed, Spanish-American War;
    discovered the cause of yellow fever
Constance Bennett, modern movie actress married to
    an air force colonel
Four McCullough brothers who fought in the Civil
    War
Over 2,000 Jewish service members, including five

The Confederate Monument at Arlington National Cemetery
Warren G. Miller, Kensington, Maryland

Gravestones of Gen. Omar Bradley, Admiral William "Bull" Halsey, Admiral William Leahy, General of the Air Force Henry "Hap" Arnold, and Gen. George Marshall
Warren G. Miller, Kensington, Maryland

Monument honoring the seven who died aboard the space shuttle *Challenger*
Warren G. Miller, Kensington, Maryland

who fought and died for the Union Army in the Civil War

482 Confederate soldiers buried in concentric circles around the Confederate Monument

Five WW II five-star officers of the U.S. military, including:

> Gen. Henry "Hap" Arnold, chief, Army Air Force
>
> Gen. Omar Bradley, chief of staff, U.S. Army
>
> Adm. William "Bull" Halsey, commander of the Pacific 3rd fleet
>
> Adm. William Leahy, chief of naval operations
>
> Gen. George Marshall, chief of staff, U.S. Army

Thirteen Afro-American Medal of Honor winners, including:

> Four from the Civil War
>
> Three from the Indian Wars
>
> Three from the Spanish-American War
>
> Three from Vietnam

Fifteen astronauts, including:

The seven commingled remains of those who died on the space shuttle *Challenger*

Lt. Virgil Grissom and Lt. Cmdr. Roger Chaffee, who died in a fire aboard their *Apollo One* spacecraft

Eight Justices of the U.S. Supreme Court, including:

William H. Taft, twenty-seventh president of the United States
Capt. Oliver Wendell Holmes
Hugo Black
Lt. Earl Warren
William O. Douglas
Potter Stewart
Arthur Joseph Goldberg
Thurgood Marshall

The monuments to these outstanding Americans and the legions of others who are not listed here stretch out beyond the horizon in every direction.

There are also many commemorative monuments spread throughout the cemetery. Some of these include:

Buffalo Soldiers Memorial. Dedicated to the memory of the Afro-American soldiers who were first mustered in 1866 and

The headstones on the graves of the *Apollo One* astronauts
Warren G. Miller, Kensington, Maryland

The official White House portrait of William H. Taft (1857–1930), twenty-seventh president of the United States

The Taft Monument at Arlington National Cemetery
Warren G. Miller, Kensington, Maryland

The Canadian Cross
Warren G. Miller, Kensington, Maryland

fought with distinction in the Spanish-American War (1898) and the Indian Wars.

USS Maine *Memorial.* The battleship USS *Maine* was blown up in Havana Harbor in 1898, killing 260 on board. Its mast stands near the graves of 229 (167 unidentified) victims of the explosion buried in the cemetery.

Nurses Memorial. A large statue of a nurse stands over the graves of hundreds of nurses who served American troops from the time of the Spanish-American War to the present.

The Confederate Monument. President Woodrow Wilson dedicated this in 1914 to make Arlington truly a national cemetery.

The Canadian Cross. Canada presented this monument to Arlington National Cemetery in 1925. It now honors the large number of U.S. citizens who enlisted in the Canadian Army and died fighting in WW I, WW II, and the Korean conflict.

The Chaplains' Monument. This was dedicated to the twenty-three chaplains who lost their lives in WW I.

Catholic Chaplains' Memorial. This commemorates the seventy Catholic chaplains who lost their lives during WW II, the six killed in the Korean War, and the seven who died in Vietnam.

Memorial Sections. There are eleven sections in the cemetery of empty graves with head-stones that read, "In the Memory of . . ." to mark the unrecovered remains of certified war dead. One of these markers is dedicated to the memory of popular "big band" leader (Alton) Glenn Miller, who disappeared in a small airplane over the English Channel in 1944.

Korean War Veterans Memorial. A memorial to honor the 54,246 who died, 8,177 missing in action, and 389 unaccounted-for prisoners of the Korean War (1950–53).

Netherlands Carillon. This is a functional concert carillon with forty-nine bells presented by the people of the Netherlands in 1954 in appreciation of the help given by the United States during and after WW II. The carillon is not located on the cemetery grounds, but on part of the adjacent Iwo Jima property.

The Lockerbie Memorial Cairn. This memorial commemorates the 259 passengers from twenty-two countries and eleven people on the ground killed by the terrorist explosion on Pan Am Flight 103 over Lockerbie, Scotland, on December 21, 1988. It is located on National Park Services land that is surrounded by the cemetery.

Sgt. Heather Lynn Johnsen, the first woman member of The Old Guard to stand guard at the Tomb of the Unknowns
Warren G. Miller, Kensington, Maryland

A section sergeant leading a black caisson unit in a funeral procession   *Courtesy of The Old Guard Caisson Platoon*

Gray caisson unit proceeding
through the cemetery (left)
*Warren G. Miller, Kensington,
Maryland*

Gray caisson unit returning to
the stables after a funeral in
Arlington National Cemetery
(below)
*Courtesy of The Old Guard
Caisson Platoon*

Ceremonial navy band leading a navy funeral at Arlington National Cemetery, 2000

Andy Garlatti, Windsor, Ontario

One of the most revered monuments at Arlington National Cemetery is the T*omb of the Unknowns,* which contains the remains of unidentified servicemen from World War I, World War II, and the Korean conflict. At one time the crypt also contained an unknown soldier from the Vietnam conflict but, when his remains were identified in 1998, they were removed and re-interred elsewhere. After that, it was agreed there would be no other Vietnam replacement in the monument. As a tribute from a thankful nation, the Tomb of the Unknowns is guarded by soldiers every hour of every day of the year.

That guard duty, as well as the responsibility for most of the military burials at the cemetery, is entrusted to the 1600 highly trained and disciplined soldiers of The Old Guard from Fort Myer. These smart-looking young men and women in their crisp blue uniforms are busy performing an average of twenty-five funerals a day with the assistance of other service honor guards.

As for Black Jack, once he had proven himself worthy of service, he was the one chosen for duty almost every time a funeral detail needed a caparisoned horse for a burial. No matter whether it was the grays or the blacks pulling the caisson, Black Jack was invariably the riderless horse prancing along behind it. The only occasions another horse was used for this purpose were the

Black Jack and his walker at
Arlington National
Cemetery
*Courtesy of The Old Guard
Caisson Platoon*

times when two funerals requiring a caparisoned horse occurred simultaneously, or when a medical condition prevented him from performing his duty.

As the months rolled by he became a fixture in Arlington National Cemetery, serving at hundreds of funerals a year. Soldiers came and went, many of the horses were replaced, but Black Jack's dramatic presence was constant.

For the first six years, Black Jack was assigned several walkers. Some he liked more than others, but in 1958 a new man came along who quickly became his favorite.

Most of the members of the Caisson Platoon came to Fort Myer as trained infantrymen or military police. Very few were expert riders. All of them had to undergo ten weeks of rigorous training both in caring for the horses and in learning to ride and handle them. On rare occasions a soldier was sent to Fort Myer who did have prior experience with horses.

One of these was a nineteen-year-old infantryman named Pete Duda, who had been raised on a farm near Ord, Nebraska, and had ridden in some local rodeos. Pete had volunteered for the

Black Jack with his walker
in front of The Old Post
Chapel at Fort Myer
Courtesy of The Old Guard
Caisson Platoon

draft in 1958 and was sent to boot camp at Fort Carson, Colorado. After finishing his basic training, he was selected for duty with The Old Guard at Fort Myer. Pete's mother, upon hearing of his appointment, made a point of proudly telling everyone she knew that her son was going to Washington to "guard the president."

Initially Pete was trained as part of the unit guarding The Tomb of the Unknowns. One day while off duty he saw a number of soldiers come by riding horses and asked his commander where they came from. When he was told they were part of the 3rd U.S. Infantry Caisson Platoon, Pete decided he wanted to join that outfit. As soon as he could, Pete walked over to the stables and told the platoon sergeant, "I want to ride these horses."

The sergeant, taken aback by Pete's blunt and unconventional approach, asked him if he had any idea about going through proper channels. Embarrassed by the sergeant's reproach, Pete went away thinking he had blown any chance to have his wish fulfilled. However, Pete's request and his trim physical build had registered with the sergeant. He must have checked out Pete's background and impeccable army record, because a few weeks later a soldier in a Jeep came by and told Pete, "C'mon, get in. You're going to shovel some horse manure."

Those few simple words articulated Pete's official transfer to The Old Guard Caisson Platoon. In due course, he was trained at every riding position and clearly demonstrated his superior horsemanship. Because Pete was so capable, he was eventually assigned to work with Black Jack and, right from the start, they established a bond that developed into a special relationship.

Pfc. Pete Duda with his "buddy," Black Jack, 1953   *Courtesy of Pete Duda*

Together they would work over 200 funerals, averaging between two and three a week. Of all the walkers who handled Black Jack over the years, Pete was possibly Black Jack's favorite.

Yet as close they were, Pete was reluctant to ride him. Whenever Pete mounted him, Black Jack lathered up with sweat so thick it looked like shaving cream. One of the few times Pete did ride him was in the winter when they were coming back to the barn late at night from a distant part of the cemetery. He and Black Jack had worked four funerals that day and Pete, whose feet were freezing from the cold, thought he would hitch a free ride back to the stables. But even in that frigid weather, when he got on Black Jack's back, the horse began to lather up in agitation. So Pete got off, and the two of them ran all the way back to the barn to keep warm. From then on, in respect for his horse, Pete resolved never to ride him again.

From the time Pete first assumed the responsibility for Black Jack, he wouldn't let anyone else go near the horse. "Nobody touches the black horse," Pete would say, "and nobody touches his leather."

When they were scheduled for a morning funeral, Pete arrived two hours before the appointed time and gave Black Jack a bath, groomed him and brushed his tail. Then he painted his hooves, saddled him and attached the appropriate insignia of the deceased's rank to the saddle blanket. To make sure Black Jack didn't get messed up while Pete got dressed in his uniform, Pete took him outside and tied him to the picket line in the corral. When the other horses were harnessed to the caisson and everyone was ready, Pete and his "buddy" moved off smartly under the direction of the section sergeant.

On the move, Pete found Black Jack high-spirited but not unmanageable. Pete says, "Although Black Jack was eleven years old at the time, he acted like a yearling." It was when they had to stop and wait that Black Jack became difficult. In front of the chapel he kicked and circled with impatience. While waiting for the service to end at the gravesite, he did the same thing. Once, while coming back from a late afternoon funeral in the dark of winter, Black Jack was at his worst. Cars heading towards them with their lights shining at him made him frantic, and Pete had all he could do to keep him under control.

The Fort Myer stables are a busy place with the horses constantly being exercised, shod, let out to pasture, drilled, and being trained with different riders. On the days when Pete wasn't walking Black Jack in a funeral, he was required to help out in the barn. Before doing so, he would take Black Jack out to the twenty-acre pasture lot south of the fort next to the marine barracks.

Then Pete would go back and help the other soldiers muck out the stalls and groom the horses in preparation for their duties in the graveyard. Often he spent up to four hours a day cleaning and polishing Black Jack's tack. At the end of his shift, Pete would go out and bring Black Jack back to the barn. As soon the horse spotted Pete coming in the distance, he would begin gently loping towards him. After a carrot or two and a brief conversation, they would begin their leisurely walk back to the stables like two old friends out on a stroll.

Together Pete and Black Jack got used to walking in all kinds of weather, from the oppressive Virginia summer humidity to the blinding winter snow. The one thing that Black Jack never learned to tolerate was the cannon salute that boomed out of nowhere, fracturing the serenity of the solemn ritual afforded to distinguished civilians and flag officers (generals and admirals with one or more stars).

In their time together, Pete Duda and Black Jack had the honor of escorting John Foster Dulles to his grave as well as an extensive number of high-ranking army officers. One of the most

Aerial view of the amphitheatre in Arlington National Cemetery with the Spanish-American War monument in the foreground   *Tom Mani, Military District of Washington Public Affairs Office*

tragic funerals they worked was a double burial of a husband and wife who were killed together in an automobile accident. Of course Black Jack couldn't distinguish the degree of sadness connected with any one ceremony. He simply performed with his usual flare on every occasion he was called upon.

Naturally the part of every ceremony he enjoyed most was his walk with Pete back to the comfort of his stall. Being deployed as often as he was, Black Jack soon came to know the turns and twists of the cemetery roads and seemed to recognize the key monuments and buildings along the way that indicated his distance from the stables.

Back in his familiar surroundings, he enjoyed being brushed and groomed and looked forward to the attention he received from his soldier friends and the treats that were offered by visitors who came to call. Every day there was a generous portion of hay at his disposal and a tasty feed of crunchy oats to enjoy.

Every six weeks Pete took him to the blacksmith shop where he stood quietly and contentedly as the farrier raised his hooves one after another and fitted his feet with a new pair of shoes.

When Pete finished his tour of duty, his departure from Fort Myer was a wrenching experience for both him and Black Jack. But Pete made it a point to come back every three weeks or so to visit his old friend. Every time he entered the barn, Black Jack seemed to recognize his voice and began kicking at the sides of his stall. Their reunions were bittersweet because they always ended with Black Jack craning his neck out over his half-door and watching Pete wave back to him as he headed out of the barn door.

Ironically it wasn't Pete Duda who would take Black Jack on his most famous walk. That would fall to another of his favorite handlers some four years down the road.

In the meantime, Black Jack satisfied himself with the company of other walkers and the contentment of his good and busy life at Fort Myer.

CHAPTER FIVE

Life at Fort Myer

FORT MYER is an extremely busy place for the Caisson Platoon as well as for the many diverse units that make the army garrison their home.

The horses are not only engaged with funerals, but are also required to participate in a variety of other activities. Because Black Jack didn't like being ridden or harnessed, he wasn't used for any of these ancillary ceremonies. His singular responsibility was serving as the platoon's caparisoned horse.

He never took part in the army retirement ceremonies where retiring military personnel are taken for a ride in the brougham coach known as the "marriage carriage." Nor was he used to pull the nineteenth-century carriage in the weddings at Fort Myer when the bride and groom leave The Old Post Chapel. He wasn't used in the historical productions presented by the 3rd U.S. Infantry Regiment, which include the annual "Spirit of America" pageant in June and the weekly summer performances of the "Torchlight Tattoo" held at the Jefferson Memorial.

He also missed the excitement of participating with the other horses in the presidential inaugural parades and the annual Memorial Day parade. He was excluded from the Fourth of July parade that marched down Constitution Avenue along the Mall, past the Lincoln Monument, the reflecting pool, and the tall spire of the Washington Monument. Although Black Jack couldn't know what he was missing, he would have enjoyed the crowds of applauding adults and cheering children who gather to see the bands, floats, and marching units, and to watch the colorful concluding ceremonies that take place on the steps of the National Archives. Then again, skittish Black Jack probably would not have enjoyed the dazzling fireworks and the flaring rockets that boom and burst over the city as darkness falls.

Caisson Platoon leader CWO5 Charles Sowles on Willie, leading the charge on Summerall Field, Fort Myer
Jim Friedman, Bedford Heights, Ohio

But the sound of music was something he was used to. The band room for The Old Guard Fife and Drum Corps is only a few buildings away from the stables, and Black Jack was accustomed to hearing them play as they rehearsed or when they marched past the barn.

Occasionally, when Black Jack was outside on the picket line, he saw them pass by in full uniform with their tall drum major leading the way in his drum major's light infantry cap, issuing commands to the bandsmen with his long ceremonial spontoon.

When the Fife and Drum Corps came by, Black Jack seemed curious about the sounds they made and the colorful clothing they wore. To this day, the drum major and the bandsmen behind him all dress in colonial uniforms—powdered wigs, white waistcoats and coveralls, red greatcoats, and black tricorn hats for the musicians. The music they make comes from the whistle of their eleven-hole fifes, the cadence of their rope-tensioned drums, and the trumpeted call of their single-valve bugles.

The Old Guard mounted unit wearing 1885 U.S. Cavalry dress uniforms for the "Spirit of America" pageant, June 2000
Laura Bonner, courtesy of The Old Guard

The Old Guard drum major leading the Fife and Drum Corps at a change-of-command ceremony on Summerall Field, Fort Myer, 2000
Charles Hickey, Essex, Ontario

An individual fife player of The Old Guard Fife and Drum Corps
Courtesy of The Old Guard

An individual drummer of The Old Guard Fife and Drum Corps
Courtesy of The Old Guard

An individual bugler of The Old Guard Fife and Drum Corps
Courtesy of The Old Guard

The Old Guard drum major leading the Fife and Drum Corps at a change-of-command ceremony on Summerall Field, Fort Myer, 2000
Peter Fillman, Toronto, Ontario

Only these instruments are used so they can genuinely reproduce the music played in the time of George Washington's Continental Army. To ensure authenticity, the tunes they play, such as "Yankee Doodle" and "British Grenadiers," have been researched and adapted from actual eighteenth-century musical arrangements.

The Fife and Drum Corps practices almost every day and marches often, because, in support of the president, they are expected to play at all armed forces arrival ceremonies for visiting dignitaries and heads of state at the White House. And their performances extend well beyond that. As an official representative of the U.S. Army, they average nearly 900 engagements a year, participating in major parades, pageants, and historical celebrations across the country as well as overseas. They also entertain at sporting events such as New Year's Day bowl games, National Basketball Association games, the Super Bowl, the Kentucky Derby, and the Indianapolis 500.

The Old Guard Fife and Drum Corps on the heights of Fort Myer overlooking Washington D.C. *Courtesy of The Old Guard*

The Old Guard Fife and Drum Corps on the march on the heights of Fort Myer overlooking Washington D.C.
Courtesy of The Old Guard

Often they are accompanied at these ceremonies by the Commander-in-Chief's Guard, a replica of "Washington's Body Guard" that was originally organized under George Washington's direct order in 1776. This sixty-six-member unit of The Old Guard, which is now stationed at nearby Fort McNair, replicates the soldiers of the Continental Army wearing uniforms similar to the Fife and Drum Corps except

Portrait of George Washington (1732–99), first president of the United States
U.S. Army Military History Institute, Carlisle, Pennsylvania

The Continental Color Guard with a unit of the 3rd U.S. Infantry Regiment (The Old Guard) in the background
Andy Garlatti, Windsor, Ontario

The Commander-in-Chief's Guard on Summerall Field, Fort Myer, 2000
Peter Fillman, Toronto, Ontario

A ceremonial unit of the U.S. Army Band "Pershing's Own" leading a funeral cortege in Arlington National Cemetery. The caisson and caparisoned horse can be seen in the background.

The U.S. Army Band, Fort Myer, Virginia

A ceremonial unit of the U.S. Army Band "Pershing's Own" in Arlington National Cemetery

The U.S. Army Band, Fort Myer, Virginia

their greatcoats are blue. Carrying twelve-pound replicas of the British Brown Bess musket fixed with thirteen-inch bayonets, they sometimes perform firing demonstrations to illustrate battle conditions during the colonial era.

Another musical unit stationed at Fort Myer is the U.S. Army Band, "Pershing's Own," which was formed in 1922 by Gen. John J. "Black Jack" Pershing. Besides participating in many tours across the U.S., the band played for the Allied troops in North Africa and Europe in World War II and was accorded a battle streamer for its efforts in boosting morale during the European Rhineland Campaign.

Black Jack often saw and sometimes heard these various marching units either separately or combined when they passed by to rehearse or perform at Conmy Hall, the indoor arena located directly across from the stables.

These three celebrated units are the most dramatic examples of the historic tradition of The Old Guard, but there is also the modern U.S. Army Drill Team, which was organized to support The Old Guard's ceremonial commitments. When not performing for the president or visiting dignitaries, the modern-clad U.S. Army Drill Team travels extensively, supporting army recruitment and acting as goodwill ambassadors for the army by participating in various military and civic functions. Besides their ceremonial obligations, members of the U.S. Army Drill Team and other regulars of the 3rd U.S. Infantry Regiment are also required to engage in tactical training to fulfill their security and military responsibilities.

As smart and modern as they look, all members of the 3rd U.S. Infantry Regiment carry a vestige of their honorable military past with them in the form of a black-and-tan buff strap on their left shoulder, a replica of the knapsack strap used by their nineteenth-century predecessors. Besides that, they are the only unit in the U.S. Army allowed to pass in review with fixed bayonets. This is a practice that was sanctioned by the War Department in honor of the 3rd U.S. Infantry's valor in the Mexican War in 1847 when they led a successful bayonet charge against the enemy at Cerro Gordo.

Although Black Jack saw soldiers or bandsmen from each of these units on a regular basis, he could not have been aware of the rich heritage that he shared with them as a member of The Old Guard Caisson Platoon.

As one of his walkers stated, "How could he know? He was smart but he was just a horse."

Nevertheless, Black Jack seemed to be aware of his own importance every time he left the barn and followed the caisson. As the years went by he mellowed somewhat but would still nip at a member of the Honor Guard if he wasn't paying attention or trod on his walker's shoes when the soldier stood too close to him.

As he grew older Black Jack became a little more tolerant about letting people on his back. Eddie Shelton, the platoon farrier, who was an experienced horse handler, occasionally rode Black Jack bareback around the turn-out lot and never had any difficulty with him. On several occasions Eddie even managed to ride him with a saddle. Still, most of the caisson riders avoided any attempt at trying to ride him.

In October 1962, Dr. Harry Rozmiarek, a twenty-three-year-old lieutenant who had just graduated from veterinary school, arrived at the stables to become the newest of the three attending army veterinarians at Fort Myer. During his tenure at the fort, it was Rozmiarek's understanding that Black Jack had trouble carrying a rider because he suffered from a weak back. However, there was not then nor is there now any known evidence that Black Jack suffered from an irregularity or a specific medical condition pertaining to his back.

During his tenure with the Caisson Platoon, young Lt. Rozmiarek experienced one of the most exciting times in his entire veterinary career. Not only did he enjoy his responsibilities with the horses, he also got to meet President John Kennedy several times as well as Jackie Kennedy and their children.

Dr. Harry Rozmiarek with the Irish deer in the quarantine facility at Fort Myer, 1963
Courtesy of Dr. Harry Rozmiarek

On one occasion he spoke to John Kennedy when the president came to Fort Myer to check on two of his Irish deer that were being quarantined there. The deer had been presented to Mr. Kennedy by the people of Ireland, and the president was very concerned about their condition and how they were getting on in their new environment.

Lt. Rozmiarek was duly impressed when the president arrived at the stables in a small convoy of black limousines with his Secret Service entourage. During his consultation with the president, Rozmiarek was even more impressed by John Kennedy's courteous manner and his sincere interest in the well-being of his two deer.

On other occasions, Rozmiarek was called out to the Kennedy family's farm at Rattlesnake Mountain near Manassas, Virginia, about a forty-minute drive from Fort Myer. On one visit, the same Irish deer that had been quarantined were showing signs of a minor respiratory problem and Lt. Rozmiarek was asked to examine them.

When he arrived at the farm, Jackie Kennedy came to greet him riding her horse with young Caroline riding alongside on her pony Macaroni. Soon after they rode up, tiny John-John made an appearance on the laneway and began undoing the shoelaces of Rozmiarek's military chauffeur who was standing at attention in Mrs. Kennedy's presence. Jackie kindly told John-John to stop pestering the driver, and he did. But moments later John-John picked up a small stone and tried to throw it at Jackie's horse—which brought another gentle reprimand from his mother.

After Rozmiarek examined the deer, Jackie asked, "Do you know what's wrong with them?"

Rozmiarek explained it was nothing more serious than the human equivalent of a cold and administered some antibiotics to the deer. Jackie expressed her relief and thanked him for his assistance. Her courtesy and genuine interest in the condition of the deer impressed the young veterinarian much the same as the president's concern when he visited the Fort Myer stables.

The most memorable meeting that Lt. Rozmiarek had with John Kennedy took place in the Oval Office when, after a consultation about one of the president's dogs, Mr. Kennedy presented him with a matchbook emblazoned with the presidential seal. The president's little gift is a prized souvenir that Harry Rozmiarek has always cherished.

Another time, Lt. Rozmiarek was taken to the emergency underground presidential headquarters by the Secret Service to inspect the food supply that was stored there. When he discovered that several tins of spaghetti had swelled, Rozmiarek condemned them and had to wait almost four hours while the agents went out and procured replacement tins. Rozmiarek then examined these new provisions and declared them safe to eat.

In May 1964, Lt. Rozmiarek was present when the Austrian government made a presentation of one of their prized milk-white Lipizzaner stallions to the Caisson Platoon. The five-year-old horse was named Conversano Beja. He was Austria's gift to America in appreciation for Gen. George S. Patton having protected the Spanish Riding School during World War II, when he made the Lipizzaners wards of the U.S. Third Army until they could be safely returned to the school at the end of the war.

The dramatic presentation took place in front of a large crowd at Madison Square Garden in New York City. At the conclusion of the Lipizzaners' performance, the lights in the arena were turned out and a spotlight followed a uniformed Austrian colonel as he rode the magnificent stallion to the center of the floor. Waiting there to accept Conversano Beja on behalf of the Old Guard was caisson platoon leader CWO4 John McKinney. After receiving the horse from the Austrian ambassador, McKinney started to mount Beja and just as he got one foot in the stirrup, the band leader shouted a command and the band struck up the first strong notes of their ceremonial music. These sharp sounds piercing the silence of the stadium startled the stallion and he reared straight up on his hind legs. As the crowd gasped in apprehension, John McKinney, the consummate horseman, didn't flinch. Without missing a beat, he continued his swing into the saddle, calmly brought Beja down on all fours, and elegantly rode off in the spotlight as the band played on.

Conversano Beja's excitable reaction that evening was soon followed by another demonstration of his volatile disposition. After the presentation ceremony, Lt. Rozmiarek, who was there to insure the horse's safe transfer to Fort Myer, helped load Beja onto a large horse trailer. Then Rozmiarek climbed aboard to accompany the great white stallion during the trip to the fort.

From the very beginning of the voyage, Conversano Beja showed clear signs of being agitated. As the trailer rolled along the New Jersey Turnpike, the horse began throwing a fit. His wildness rapidly escalated to such a fever pitch that the trailer began to rock from side to side. On Rozmiarek's orders, the driver pulled the trailer over to the shoulder of the highway and parked. Conversano Beja continued his unruly behavior for another ten minutes or so, but then, as Rozmiarek predicted, he eventually wore himself out and settled down. Once he was calm and under control again, the journey was completed with no further incidents.

But Conversano Beja's wild display of temperament was an omen of more erratic behavior to come. The worst of these episodes occurred when he was on parade in Washington and somehow managed to break free and jump into the Tidal Basin, the large body of water between the Jefferson Memorial and the Washington Monument. Although the pool is only some three and a half feet deep, there are no steps anywhere around it that would afford the horse an exit.

Consequently, Conversano Beja had to stand for hours in the water cooled by the evening breeze while Chief McKinney sent for a crane to lift the horse out of the Tidal basin. While they waited for the derrick, McKinney, dressed as George Washington, and other Old Guard personnel in full dress blues, jumped into the water to comfort and calm the unpredictable stallion. Finally the crane arrived and technicians from Fort Myer had to enter the water and secure bands around the horse's belly to extricate him. By the time Conversano Beja was lifted out and deposited safely on dry land, he was so cramped and tired he could barely stand. He had to be trailered back to the stables and it was days before he was fit for service.

During all the time that Conversano Beja and Black Jack were together at Fort Myer, Black Jack always seemed wary of the unpredictable Lipizzaner and wanted little to do with him.

Although Black Jack never warmed to Conversano Beja, he seemed to make close friendships with some of his other stablemates. One he really liked was a beautiful gray named Sonoma who had the stall next to him. A huge horse standing 16 hands and weighing 1,400 pounds, Sonoma was a smart, attractive, alpha mare with a forceful character that dominated the other horses in the barn. Black Jack showed no signs of jealousy with strong-willed Sonoma and the two of them got along well. Often they were seen standing nose-to-nose peering at each other through the bars of their stalls.

However, another horse that Black Jack didn't seem to care for was a later arrival named Shorty. Like Black Jack, Shorty was a jet-black horse of similar conformation brought to the fort to be used exclusively as the alternate caparisoned horse.

Although Shorty was sharp and handsome, he soon showed signs of being crazy. At one time or another he either kicked or bit just about every rider in the barn. Sometimes he behaved properly; but then, without any apparent reason he went wild and kicked at his stall in a frenzy. During one demented spell Shorty kicked so hard and so often with his rear hooves that he eventually broke

Eddie Shelton, the farrier, with Conversano Beja. Black Jack is standing behind them, 1968.   *Courtesy of Eddie Shelton*

CWO4 John McKinney riding Conversano Beja out of Madison Square Garden after accepting him from the Austrian government, May, 1964. In the background the Colonial Color Guard is flanked by members of The Old Guard.

Courtesy of the McKinney family

through the two layers of brick that form the stable's exterior wall. In an attempt to stop him from doing this, the farrier removed his rear shoes, but Shorty kept right on kicking until his rear hocks swelled so badly he became lame. He suffered that way for almost a month.

After seeing and hearing Shorty in action, Black Jack wanted no part of him, and the feeling seemed to be mutual. That worked out fine for both horses because their paths seldom crossed. They always worked alone and only went out of the barn at the same time when there were two separate funerals being held simultaneously.

In a way, Shorty's arrival signaled the beginning of a new era in the stables; Black Jack was getting older, and the young and frisky Shorty was obviously his heir apparent. Black Jack couldn't have known this, and he certainly didn't register any complaints about his workload being reduced. Each trip that Shorty worked meant one less assignment into the cemetery for Black Jack.

On rare occasions there was controversy concerning the horses at Fort Myer. In the mid-1950s, the secretary of defense ordered a study that concluded horse-drawn funerals were considerably more expensive than those using motorized hearses. As a result, an order was issued by the army vice-chief of staff to abolish forthwith all horse-drawn funerals. However, when this decree was made known, the public reaction against it was so swift and pronounced that several congressmen openly opposed it. Venerable Gen. George Marshall, one-time chief of staff and former secretary of defense, vehemently disagreed with the new order and phoned his old friend President Eisenhower at the White House to complain. The president immediately intervened and ordered the horse-drawn funerals to continue. That ended that.

A few years later, an unsettling situation developed at the stables concerning the gray horses. Because matched grays were becoming increasingly difficult to acquire, the army administration considered the idea of gradually

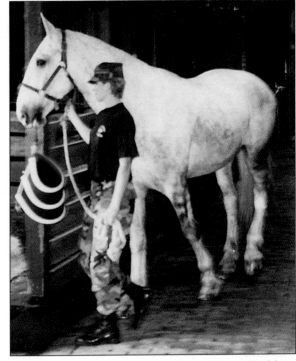

A gray being led to his stall in The Old Guard stables, 2000 *Ray Kosi, Newport Beach, California*

Black Jack and his
walker, Pfc. John
Kwiatkowski, at
Arlington National
Cemetery, winter 1968
*The U.S. Army,
courtesy of
The Old Guard*

eliminating them from the caisson unit. This would have meant that a number of Black Jack's old friends would be sent away.

However, once again, when the public discovered that such a plan was a possibility, many civilians and military personnel became upset and raised objections. This mini-crisis was averted when the administration of the Caisson Platoon decided to modify their plans by reducing the grays' workload and creating two separate units of blacks and grays that would work alternate weeks.

Of course Black Jack knew nothing of these matters but he surely would have been upset to lose some of his gray friends before their departure time was due. Nevertheless, blithely unaware of anything but his own little world, Black Jack continued to perform in his lively way on a reduced schedule that meant all the more often he was kept warm and comfortable in the cozy confines of his stall.

One issue that did seem to be of paramount importance to him was the selection of the man assigned to be his walker. Black Jack's handlers were replaced approximately every eighteen months when their respective tours of duty were completed. All of these men, including John Best, John Kwiatkowski, Paul Minugh, Tom Chapman, and Ronald Richards were particularly good to him; Pete Duda, the Nebraska farm boy, was exceptional.

But in early 1963, a new private named Arthur Anders Carlson transferred to the 3rd U.S. Infantry Regiment and soon after was assigned to the Caisson Platoon. Within weeks Arthur Carlson became Black Jack's new walker.

A few months after their pairing, the two of them together would make the most significant journey of their lives.

Black Jack with his walker, 1974
The U.S. Army, courtesy of The Old Guard

CHAPTER SIX

Arthur A. Carlson

ALTHOUGH ARTHUR CARLSON had no qualifications for working with horses, he soon learned the knack of dealing with them. Born in Foley, Alabama, he volunteered for the army at eighteen years of age and was shipped out to Fort Gordon in Georgia for basic training. When he heard that The Old Guard was looking for candidates who were neat in appearance and stood between 5'10" and 6'6", he decided to apply. Being handsome, 6'2" and a lean 170 pounds, his application was accepted and within days he was notified to report to Fort Myer in Virginia.

Arthur arrived at the fort on a Friday evening and, with little to do, he and another new recruit, Jerry Bird from West Virginia, decided to go for a walk around the base. When they came across the stables, they went in and spoke to a couple of soldiers from the Caisson Platoon and quickly came to the conclusion that working there would be better than serving with an honor guard or marching all day with a rifle slung over their shoulders.

The following Monday they went back to the stables and spoke to CWO4 John McKinney, the man in charge of the Caisson Platoon, which was then called the Caisson Section. McKinney was an experienced hand with military animals. He not only was the senior member serving at the stables, he was also a World War II veteran who had fought in the jungles of Burma with a mule-drawn, pack howitzer unit.

Both Carlson and Bird expressed their interest in joining the Caisson Section, and after a short but informative conversation, Mr. McKinney took their names and told them he would let them know about the possibility of their transferring to his unit.

The next day a sergeant came by their quarters and told both Carlson and Bird, "Get your gear together, you're going over to the Caisson Section."

Pfc. Arthur A. Carlson with Black Jack, 1963 · · · · · · · The U.S. Army, *courtesy of Arthur Carlson*

During his first three weeks at the stables Carlson was put to work cleaning the stalls. After that, he rode the swing pair for a couple of days. Because of his height, build, and appearance, as soon as he demonstrated he was good with the horses, Mr. McKinney told Carlson he was assigning him to replace Pfc. Red McKinnon, a Canadian whose tour of duty was ended, to be Black Jack's walker. In that same conversation, McKinney warned Carlson never to ride him.

"He's got very small hooves and can be easily injured," McKinney said. "He doesn't like any weight on him. So don't ride that horse."

With that warning in mind, Carlson was surprised to find that working with Black Jack was not difficult. Possibly that was because Black Jack, now in middle age, was less excitable and somewhat easier to handle than he had been previously. During their first few months serving together from Monday to Friday, Arthur Carlson and Black Jack worked one or two funerals a day.

A little after one-thirty in the afternoon on November 22, Carlson was about to leave his residence when he heard on the radio that President Kennedy had been shot in Dallas. He hurried over to the stables and went into the CQ room, a small lounge where the riders took their breaks. Almost every soldier of the Caisson Section was in there with his attention riveted on the television set. Shortly after Arthur got there, the president was pronounced dead. Even though the soldiers were shaken by the announcement, they all knew their unit would be integrally involved in the president's funeral, and turned to Chief McKinney for their initial preparations.

McKinney decided they should use the same caisson that had carried President Roosevelt to his grave in 1945. A "white-horse squad" was selected that included Cloud Burst and Tap as the wheel

CWO4 John McKinney astride Big Boy, the section horse used in President Kennedy's funeral   *Courtesy of Dr. Harry Rozmiarek*

pair with Blue and Blue Dare as the lead pair. The swing pair would be Rocket and Prince. Although Mr. McKinney realized that Rocket was unpredictable, he figured if they used him as the off-horse, Prince and his rider would be able to keep him in line. Sgt. Tom Setterberg was assigned as the section sergeant; Big Boy was chosen as the section horse. Black Jack was the clear choice for the "cap" horse.

After the horses were chosen, Mr. McKinney selected the riders. It was automatic that Arthur Carlson would be Black Jack's walker.

Then everyone set to work cleaning tack, shining brass, and getting their uniforms ready. The platoon had lots of time to prepare because they soon learned that the first day they would be involved in the funeral arrangements would be Sunday, November 24.

That Sunday morning Arthur reported to the stables at six a.m. First he checked out Black Jack, particularly his feet. Then he groomed him, inspected his tack, and put on his own uniform, which was freshly cleaned and pressed. After that he saddled Black Jack, fitted him with the dangling ceremonial sword, and inserted gleaming black cavalry boots backwards in the stirrups. When the grays were harnessed to the caisson and the unit was ready to move out, Carlson led Black Jack to the rear of the stables and formed up behind the ceremonial wagon.

On the section sergeant's command the unit departed and began the long three-mile walk through the cemetery, across the Memorial Bridge over the Potomac, and through the city to the Treasury Building on Pennsylvania Avenue. The plan was for them to wait there until an appointed time so there would be no problem arriving at the White House on schedule.

The only difficulty along the way was that occasionally the brisk pace of the caisson had to be slowed down so that Arthur and Black Jack could catch up. Other than that, all along the route Black Jack was calm and steady and not the least bit of trouble.

However, at the Treasury Building an incident occurred that would have lasting repercussions over the next two days. When the unit was about to leave the quadrangle for the White House through a vehicular tunnel onto the street, the right rear wheel of the caisson got stuck in a slot in a huge eight-by-four-foot gutter grate in the tunnel. It was so firmly jammed in the slot that the caisson dragged the iron grate against the stone wall and over the cobbled roadway for a number of yards, making a horrible grinding sound that seemed to unnerve all the horses—but particularly Black Jack.

Carlson says, "From that moment on, Black Jack seemed to decide to act like he was spooked for the next two days."

When the unit arrived at the White House, Black Jack behaved badly. He was slobbering at the mouth and wouldn't stand still. He kept tossing his head and swishing his tail, and he started dancing around so that he was facing Carlson with his rear to the caisson. After that, as the muffled drums repeated their somber cadence down Pennsylvania Avenue to Constitution Avenue over to Delaware Avenue, Black Jack tugged at his lead strap and pranced around nervously, sometimes almost sideways, all the way to the Capitol.

At the Capitol Building, when the pallbearers removed the coffin from the caisson and carried it up the steps into the rotunda, Black Jack started sweating until he was soaked and, once again, began dancing around fretfully. Protocol dictated that Arthur was not to talk to his horse while in public, and he didn't. In hindsight, he now thinks he should have spoken to Black Jack in an attempt to settle him down.

Black Jack and Arthur Carlson behind the caisson departing the White House for the Capitol, November 24, 1963
The John F. Kennedy Library, Boston

On the way back to the stables, once again the caisson kept getting away from Carlson and Black Jack, and several times it had to slow down to let them catch up. The trip both ways was a long walk and during all that time neither Black Jack nor Arthur Carlson had so much as a drink of water. This Spartan regimen applied to every person engaged in the cortege as well as all the

Arthur Carlson and Black Jack leaving the grounds of the White House, November 24, 1963
The John F. Kennedy Library, Boston

members of the military that lined both sides of the streets. As difficult as this was for everyone involved, Carlson knew that come Monday the procession would be even longer and more demanding.

When they got back to the stables, Arthur unsaddled Black Jack, cleaned and groomed him with a currycomb and brush, then settled him in his stall.

In the CQ room the soldiers who had not been involved in the president's cortege told Arthur they had watched the ceremony on television and informed him that the announcers had talked repeatedly about both him and Black Jack. Then, the unit that had been in the funeral procession

The caisson at the Capitol. Jackie, Bobby, and the Kennedy children are in the background to the right

The John F. Kennedy Library, Boston

watched reruns of the event on television and discussed what was good about their performance and what they needed to improve for the next day.

"We very much wanted to do this the best we could," says Carlson. "We were focused on that."

On Monday, the day of the funeral, the caisson unit was in a frenzy. Not only did they have to attend to John Kennedy's final procession, there were twenty-three other funerals that had been scheduled for that day at Arlington National Cemetery!

For Carlson and the rest of the president's burial team, the routine was basically the same as the previous day, except this time the long walk from the stables was directly to the Capitol Building.

In the procession from the Capitol to the White House, Black Jack was even less cooperative than he had been the day before. All along the route he tugged violently on the lead strap, and was so difficult to handle that Arthur was afraid he would lose hold of him.

Over and over in his mind he kept repeating to himself, "Please God don't let this horse get away from me. Please don't let him get away."

Carlson knew if Black Jack ever got free and bolted, the army would ship him, Arthur, to a radar shack on the Distant Early Warning line somewhere up in Greenland.

The handler of the caparisoned horse is required to walk ramrod straight with his eyes focused solely on the caisson ten feet ahead. However, when the caisson unit reached the White House, and the horde of dignitaries began filling in behind the Kennedys—who were directly behind Black Jack—Arthur couldn't help but notice two distinguished heads of state. One was Charles de Gaulle, the other Haile Selassie. These two stood out because they were both in uniform; and de Gaulle was so tall while Selassie, walking close by him, was so tiny. Other than these two personages, Carlson had no idea who was following behind him.

At St. Matthew's Cathedral, while the caisson unit waited for the requiem mass to end, Black Jack started to act up again. Carlson was standing at parade rest, anchoring his horse, when Black Jack began pawing the ground. In the process, Black Jack stepped on Carlson's right big toe so hard that Arthur was sure it was broken. What made matters worse, Carlson couldn't bend down to rub it and dared not shed a tear in front of the bank of television cameras.

"I would have liked to had a heart-to-heart talk with him about his behavior. I would have told him a thing or two in detail."

Arthur Carlson and Black Jack waiting for President Kennedy's casket to descend the Capitol steps, November 25, 1963

The John F. Kennedy Library, Boston

Instead, Carlson extended his arm, holding the lead strap out from his body to keep Black Jack further from his damaged foot. As soon as they began marching away from the cathedral, it took all of Arthur's resolve to walk without showing any signs of pain.

Of the various segments in the processions for John Kennedy, the most memorable for Carlson was the trip from the church to Arlington National Cemetery. One of the sounds that he still remembers most vividly from that time so long ago is the skirl of the bagpipes.

An impatient Black Jack waiting as President Kennedy's casket is borne to the caisson outside the Capitol

The John F. Kennedy Library, Boston

Black Jack moving about impatiently in front of the White House as the dignitaries wait to fall in behind the Kennedys for the funeral procession to St. Matthew's Cathedral   *The John F. Kennedy Library, Boston*

Black Jack restless and foaming at the mouth outside St. Matthew's Cathedral

The John F. Kennedy Library, Boston

"That's music to fight by," he says. "It kept me going, infused me with energy."

Another sound that still haunts him is the steady thumping of the muffled drums playing the same deliberate rhythm over and over again.

Reflecting on that leg of the journey, he says, "The rattling of the caisson's iron wheels on the pavement, the drums, the pipes, the clip-clop of the horses' hooves on the pavement—it all comes back to me now and then."

Oddly, it was the *absence of sound* that left him with the most lasting impression.

"I had to keep my eyes straight ahead. But out of the corner of my eye I could see the sides of the streets were packed solid with people. But they were completely quiet. They didn't even seem to move. And they didn't make a sound. I really remember that."

The caisson unit and limousines heading for Arlington National Cemetery   *The John F. Kennedy Library, Boston*

Black Jack and Arthur Carlson marching down Pennsylvania Avenue in John Kennedy's funeral, November 25, 1963
The U.S. Army, courtesy of Nancy Schado

On the way to the graveyard, Black Jack continued to misbehave but he and Carlson had less trouble keeping up with the caisson.

"It was a slow walking pace. I just had to make sure I kept my distance from the Navy Seaman carrying the president's flag in front of me. The one thing I did see was the Custis-Lee mansion on the hill straight ahead of us as we crossed the Arlington Memorial Bridge over the Potomac."

Jackie Kennedy after receiving her husband's burial flag at the interment service in Arlington National Cemetery
The John F. Kennedy Library, Boston

To honor Jacqueline Kennedy's special request, The Old Guard Fife and Drum Corps stood waiting on the lawn near the entrance to the cemetery. They didn't play a note, but their colorful colonial uniforms added a special touch to the ceremonies and was a final reminder of their unflinching loyalty to the president.

When the caisson arrived at the gravesite, Carlson and an impatient Black Jack waited on the roadway while the pallbearers took the coffin off the caisson and carried it up the incline. After the Marine Band played the national anthem, the Air Force Pipers began a slow march past the gravesite playing "Mist Covered Mountain."

By then, the gray horses and Black Jack had rolled out and were once again weaving their way through the cemetery on the roads they knew so well leading them back to their stables.

After the horses were cared for, the soldiers from the funeral procession went into the CQ room and again viewed their performance on TV replays. Carlson remembers watching his posture visibly degrade from tiredness as the procession neared the bridge over the Potomac.

"It was physically exhausting," he says. "There was a lot of walking and I was tired. When we were going over that bridge, I really thought I was going to lose it."

But he didn't. And during those two remarkable days of walking, he and Black Jack carved out a niche in history that can never be erased. It's one of the accomplishments in Arthur Carlson's life that he neither asked for nor designed. Nor is it something he thinks of as a famous feat.

Black Jack and Arthur Carlson follow President Kennedy's caisson into Arlington National Cemetery. The Old Guard Fife and Drum Corps stands at attention on the far right. *U.S. Navy via the John F. Kennedy Library, Boston*

"It was just a job I had to do. That was a terrible time for all of us, a pretty serious time. There was no praise for us, or anything like that. We were all pretty down."

A day or two after John Kennedy's funeral, he and Black Jack were back at work in Arlington National Cemetery. During their time together, by Arthur Carlson's recorded count, they participated in ninety-four funerals. Only one other of those honored a national celebrity and that would occur four months in the future.

Black Jack and Arthur Carlson stand and wait near the gravesite as President Kennedy's coffin is removed from the caisson

U.S. Navy via the John F. Kennedy Library, Boston

CHAPTER SEVEN

Celebrity

THE EXTENSIVE media coverage of John Kennedy's funeral carried the image of Black Jack around the world. Readers and viewers were not only impressed with his beauty and the historic ritual he represented, they were very much taken by the spirit he displayed. Black Jack's dash and temperament seemed to strike a responsive chord in many Americans who had admired similar qualities in their dead president's character. One of the people who came to admire Black Jack's qualities was Jacqueline Kennedy herself.

Mrs. Kennedy was a deeply sensitive and private woman. Accompanied by Bobby Kennedy, she had returned unannounced to her husband's grave at midnight on the day of his burial to place a sprig of flowers at the foot of his grave. The next day the media were advised that Mrs. Kennedy wished to remain in seclusion for a few days.

However, on November 27, Jackie informed the secretary of the army, via her husband's military aide, that she wanted to buy Black Jack after the horse had completed his service to the army and was ready for retirement. By a matter of mere coincidence, Jacqueline Kennedy's father, John Vernon Bouvier III, was nicknamed "Black-Jack" supposedly because of his penchant for gambling.

Mrs. Kennedy's request to purchase Black Jack was acknowledged and she was informed that this would be possible some time in the future when Black Jack's active career was ended.

Soon after that, in a symbolic gesture, the army presented Black Jack's caparison to Mrs. Kennedy. This included the bridle, saddle, saddle blanket, sword, boots and spurs.

The horseshoes that Black Jack wore the day of the funeral had been taken off as soon as he got back to the barn and were given to Dr. Harry Rozmiarek, one of the platoon veterinarians at that time.

Not long after President Kennedy's funeral, a woman named Nancy Schado became avidly interested in Black Jack. She had watched every moment of the ceremonies on television and, although deeply saddened by their impact, she was captivated by Black Jack's style and beauty.

Married to an army colonel living near Fort Myer, Nancy had a longtime association with the military. Her first husband, Woodrow Lane, had been a radio operator on a B-29 and was killed in 1945 on a bombing run over Tokyo. Jack Wentworth, her second husband, was a captain in the Army Medical Corps and served at Walter Reed Hospital in Washington. They were married five years and then divorced. Ten years after that marriage dissolved, Nancy wed Col. Michael Schado, who had gone ashore with the troops on D-Day at Normandy and later served in Korea. When Michael Schado was assigned to his duties at the Pentagon, he and Nancy had taken up residence in Arlington, Virginia.

Nancy was a very active woman with many interests. One of her more time-consuming pastimes was serving as the chairwoman with the Army Arlington Ladies. This association assigns one of its members to every military funeral held in Arlington National Cemetery to commiserate with the family of the deceased. The member attends the burial, presents the family with sympathy cards, and often makes arrangements for having flowers put on the grave. Sometimes an Arlington Lady is the only person in attendance at a burial.

Nancy Schado also had a passion for animals. She often dropped by the stables at Fort Myer to visit the horses but had never spent any time with Black Jack. After seeing him participate in the president's funeral procession, she made a mental note to meet him.

Shortly after the president's funeral, Nancy went to the barns to feed the horses a few apples and carrots. While petting one of them, she asked Pete Cote, the blacksmith, "Which horse is the one who followed the president's caisson in the funeral procession?"

Pete answered, "He's the one you're petting."

"So you're Black Jack," Nancy said as she stroked his nose. "You're even more beautiful than you appeared on television."

Nancy spent the remainder of her time at the stables that day talking to Black Jack, rubbing his nose, and patting his neck.

That first meeting was the beginning of a beautiful and long-lasting friendship. Every week, either on a Tuesday or Wednesday, Nancy baked a cake for the soldiers in the caisson unit and always saved a generous portion for Black Jack.

When Nancy came to realize that Black Jack's favorite flavor was butter pecan, she baked nothing but that. As time went on, whenever Black Jack heard Nancy's voice or sensed her presence entering the barn, he kicked the side of his stall in anticipation, just like he'd done with his former walker, Pete Duda.

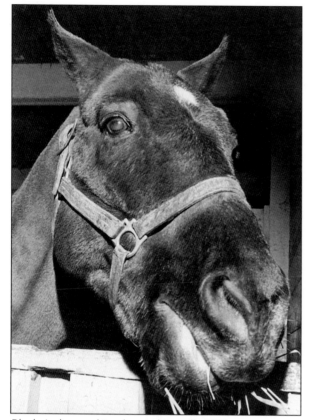

Black Jack munching hay in his stall, 1973
The U.S. Army, courtesy of Nancy Schado

When the Caisson Platoon leader, CWO4 John McKinney, learned of Nancy's devotion to the horse, he dubbed her "Black Jack's Mother," a title she still relishes with pride.

Nancy came to see Black Jack often, but she wasn't the only visitor he had at the barn. Because of Black Jack's renown as the riderless horse in John Kennedy's funeral, school children soon began to arrive at the caisson stables. At first they came in ones and twos with their parents or grandparents. Before long, they began to arrive by the busload. Teachers, realizing that Black Jack was a national treasure and a symbol of patriotism, brought their pupils to the stables so they could see and touch the horse who had followed their beloved president to his grave.

Some weeks as many as 200 children visited the barns to pet the country's most famous military horse. And Black Jack never failed to impress them. He seemed especially to love children and responded to their affection with animation.

Occasionally visitors to the barn asked if they could have one of Black Jack's horseshoes as a souvenir. At first these requests were few and easily accommodated because Black Jack was re-shod every six weeks. But gradually the demand for his shoes increased and the practice of supplying them became a problem.

Such was the case when a nun in her black habit came to the stables and asked a soldier if she could have one of Black Jack's shoes for the children in her school. The farrier, who was reluctant to break up the one spare set he had, declined the request, so the soldier gave the nun a shoe from another horse. She immediately went outside where Black Jack was tied up and lifted his foot to measure the shoe on his hoof. When she saw that the shoe in her possession was too big for Black Jack, she hurried back to the rider to question its authenticity.

Embarrassed by being caught in a deception, the soldier had little choice but to appeal to the farrier to give her one of Black Jack's real shoes. When he agreed, the nun went out and tried that horseshoe on for size and, being satisfied it fit, came back to the soldier and whispered, "The children will love this. God bless you, my son."

Then she hurried out of the barn with her prized trophy in hand, leaving the young rider to regret his deceit.

Early in 1964, Black Jack was assigned to serve in the funeral of another national hero. In April of that year, General of the Army Douglas MacArthur passed away at Walter Reed Hospital. Since President Kennedy had previously authorized a state funeral in the general's honor, President Johnson confirmed that directive by ordering that the old soldier be buried "with all the honor a grateful nation can bestow on a departed hero."

Plans for the funeral, which had been made in consultation with the general himself, specified that the ceremonies should extend over seven days. His body was to lie in state at the 7th Regiment Armory in New York City, then at the Capitol in Washington, and finally in the MacArthur Memorial Building in Norfolk, Virginia, where he was to be entombed.

These complex arrangements caused some concern for the Caisson Platoon because they had to supply a caisson unit and a riderless horse for all three occasions on a very tight schedule.

Chief McKinney decided to use a black horse section with Shorty as the riderless horse in New York and then have that unit trucked directly to Norfolk so they could perform their duties there. In between those two ceremonies, another unit of grays was to serve in the Washington procession with Black Jack as the riderless horse. The Caisson Platoon leader's intention was to limit the demands on Black Jack, who by this time was seventeen years old.

General of the Army Douglas MacArthur (1880–1964)
The MacArthur Memorial Library and Archives, Norfolk, Virginia

To put his decision in perspective, it should be remembered that a horse's age is multiplied by three-and-a-half to compare it to the age of a human being. This meant that Black Jack was now going on sixty in human terms. Shorty was chosen for the double duty because, being much younger, he could better cope with the rigors of travel.

Besides that, Black Jack had never been trucked or trailered, and the platoon leader didn't want to put him under this kind of stress in the twilight of his career.

It was automatic that Arthur Carlson would be Black Jack's walker in Washington. Although Carlson had worked with Shorty before and had learned how to keep him under control, his first responsibility was to Black Jack. Pfc. James Stimpson from Munford, Tennessee, was assigned the task of walking Shorty both in New York and Norfolk.

As it turned out, Mr. McKinney's logistics were sound. The black caisson unit and Shorty departed in a twelve-horse van for New York on April 5 at 10:30 p.m. and didn't arrive until 5:30 a.m. the next morning. They were housed at the Park Police stables in New York City for the day, and the next morning at eight a.m. they set off on the two-and-a-half-mile procession to Pennsylvania Station. As soon as the general's body was transferred to the train, the black caisson unit was reloaded on the van for the trip to Norfolk.

The loading took place in a roped-off area on 5th Avenue and all went well until they tried to board a horse named Oscar. For some reason, Oscar refused to go up the ramp into the van. As soon as his front feet touched the ramp he repeatedly reared up and became uncontrollable. Each time this happened the large crowd that had gathered to watch the loading let out a loud cheer, which only made matters worse. The soldiers tried everything to get him up the ramp, including putting a jacket over Oscar's head to blind him, but nothing worked. Finally, veterinarian Harry Rozmiarek, who was traveling with the caisson unit, gave Oscar a mild tranquilizer to calm him

Shorty parading at Gen. MacArthur's funeral in Norfolk, Virginia, 1964
The U.S. Army, courtesy of Nancy Schado

Black Jack following Gen. MacArthur's casket in Washington, April 1964

The MacArthur Memorial Library and Archives, Norfolk, Virginia

Black Jack follows
Gen. MacArthur's
coffin as it departs the
Capitol, April 1964
*The MacArthur
Memorial Library and
Archives, Norfolk,
Virginia*

down. Momentarily, when the sedative took effect, Oscar became more tractable and was led up
the ramp without any further difficulty.

However, during his several wild episodes on the ramp, Oscar had cut himself and needed to
be sutured by Lt. Rozmiarek before the unit departed for Norfolk. By then it was 11:30 a.m. and
there was another long drive ahead.

The entire trip from Fort Myer to New York to Norfolk would have been a taxing experience
for Black Jack, and it was wise that he wasn't involved in these two separated segments of the
MacArthur ceremonies.

When Gen. MacArthur's coffin arrived in Washington it was borne by hearse to Constitution
Avenue and 16th Street where it was transferred to the gray caisson unit. From there, Black Jack
followed the caisson to the Capitol in a colorful cortege that included a national color detail, an
honor guard, clergy, bands, and a host of marching units. Predictably, all along the route Black
Jack was as spirited as ever.

Black Jack outside the Capitol at Gen. MacArthur's funeral in Washington, D.C., April 1964
The U.S. Army and The Old Guard Museum, Fort Myer, Virginia

In the light rain of April 9, Black Jack returned to the Capitol Building with the gray unit to escort the general's casket in a procession along Constitution Avenue to 14th Street, where it was transferred to a hearse and taken to Washington National Airport for the flight to Norfolk. By tradition, the caparisoned horse only follows a caisson, never a motorized hearse.

As soon as the hearse and the other limousines in the cortege departed for the airport, Arthur Carlson and Black Jack began their long walk back to the stables. Once again they had been the focus of international media attention and Black Jack's reputation was enhanced even more. Photos of him prancing along behind the caisson were on the front pages of many newspapers in America and some overseas.

The visitors to the stables continued to come daily, and Nancy Schado never missed a week when she didn't drop by with a piece of butter pecan cake and a few loving words for her "Sweetie Pie," as she called him. Many times she came to the stables two or three times a week to kiss him, rub noses with him, or get him to take a sugar cube from between her lips.

Black Jack's best friend Raven with his walker in Arlington National Cemetery
Courtesy of The Military District of Washington

As their relationship developed, Black Jack seemed to become possessive of Nancy and showed his displeasure when she shared his apple pieces with the other horses, even with his old pal Sonoma and a more recent friend named Raven.

As close as Black Jack and Sonoma seemed to be, when Raven arrived at the barn, he soon became Black Jack's very best friend. Raven and Black Jack had a lot in common. Both stood 15.1 hands and weighed around 1,150 pounds. Both were jet black with stars on their foreheads, except Raven had a white sock on his left rear foot. And both of them were used exclusively as caparisoned horses. Still, Black Jack didn't like sharing Nancy's treats with either Raven or Sonoma.

One of the horses in the barn that Black Jack continued to eye with suspicion was the Lipizzaner Conversano Beja. Any time Nancy went near Conversano Beja, Black Jack seemed to show his annoyance by stomping around in his stall and making a ruckus to attract her attention. And when Nancy brought apples or carrots, Black Jack's behavior made it very clear that he was not prepared to share them with Conversano Beja.

Nancy's visits with Black Jack were such a preoccupation that her husband began wondering why she was spending so much time visiting a horse. To circumvent his objections, she started making up excuses so she could make trips to the fort that would allow her to visit the stables. On one occasion when her husband was about to become angry with her for doing this, Nancy told him, "Go ahead and get mad. I don't care. I'll move into a stall with Black Jack."

Seven months after Gen. MacArthur's burial, Black Jack escorted another ex-president in a high-profile funeral procession in Washington. This time it was ninety-year-old Herbert Hoover, who had died on October 20, 1964, in his suite at the Waldorf Astoria Hotel in New York City.

Interestingly enough, the caisson unit had been prepared to transport their horses by air to Iowa where Mr. Hoover was to be buried. On veterinarian Rozmiarek's recommendation they had rehearsed the logistics of the transfer by trucking the horses to Andrews Air Force Base, loading them onto a transport plane, and flying over Chesapeake Bay for about twenty minutes to make sure all concerned—especially the horses—were familiar with the entire air transfer process. However, when Herbert Hoover died, his original funeral plans were changed and the caisson unit was not required to attend in Iowa.

Mr. Hoover's funeral was held on October 22 at St. Bartholomew's Episcopal Church in New York City. On the 23rd, his body was taken to Pennsylvania Station for transfer to Washington. Black Jack's services were required to escort his coffin from the train station in Washington to the Capitol.

Portrait sketch of Herbert Hoover (1874–1964), thirty-first president of the United States

Herbert Hoover Presidential Library, West Branch, Iowa

For this procession, Black Jack was not walked by Arthur Carlson because, by then, he had completed his tour of duty.

The caisson unit and Black Jack met the train at Union Station and escorted Hoover's casket to the Capitol in a long cortege of marching units and bands under the command of Col. Joseph Conmy, Jr. In years to come, the arena across from the caisson stables would bear the colonel's name and be known as Conmy Hall.

After lying in state for one day, Mr. Hoover's remains were taken by hearse to the airport for a flight to his hometown, West Branch, Iowa, where he was to be buried. Although a caisson unit was not involved in this final procession, Black Jack had now served in the funerals of three persons of international renown.

In 1967, when Black Jack was twenty years old, he suffered a bowed tendon in his leg, but with care he recovered and before long was sound again. However, this injury and the administration's concern for his advancing age caused them to consider retiring him to the 200-

Black Jack and the caisson unit bearing Herbert Hoover's coffin arriving at the Capitol, October 1964
Herbert Hoover Presidential Library, West Branch, Iowa

Black Jack misbehaving as Herbert Hoover's casket is borne up the steps to the Capitol, 1964
Herbert Hoover Presidential Library, West Branch, Iowa

acre Army Animal Facility at Fort Meade, Maryland. Before doing that, the secretary of the army sent a letter to Jackie Kennedy, asking if she was still interested in purchasing him.

In part, the letter stated:

Black Jack is now of the age and physical condition which will necessitate his retirement from active Federal service. Thus, if you are still interested in acquiring him, necessary measures will be taken to complete the transaction. In the event, however, that you do not wish to purchase him at this time, he will be retired to the well-equipped Animal Facility of the Army Institute of Research at Fort Meade, Maryland, where you can be assured he will be comfortable but not subjected to research activities.

I would appreciate being apprised of your decision on this matter.

Mrs. Kennedy replied:

Dear Mr. Secretary,

I do want to thank you for your letter of July 14th and I was so touched that you wrote me about Black Jack.

I have been thinking it over and it does seem that Black Jack would be happiest if retired to the Army animal division at Fort Meade. I know he would get the very best of care there and that is what is most important to me.

Thank you so much for remembering my interest in Black Jack and I am so pleased to know he will be well taken care of for the rest of his years.

With my best wishes,

Sincerely
(signed) Jacqueline Kennedy

Having been apprised of Mrs. Kennedy's wishes and because Black Jack still seemed strong and vibrant, the army decided to defer his retirement but reduce his work load. His lightened responsibilities provided Black Jack with a well-deserved rest. By the end of 1967 he had participated in more than 1,000 ceremonial funeral processions.

On January 19, 1968, Nancy Schado gave Black Jack his first birthday party. She encouraged the army to help publicize the event and managed to get photos of Black Jack and articles about his birthday celebration in the *Pentagram News* as well as several other newspapers in the Washington area.

Nancy baked him a butter pecan cake and bought him a bag of carrots and apples as well. On top of the cake she placed a little toy horse that she had purchased from a drug store in Arlington, Virginia. Nancy painted it black with a white star on its forehead, and even went so far as to add a tiny saddle and little black boots reversed in the stirrups.

The party was held in front of a large number of invited guests and curious onlookers in the parking lot outside the stables. The highlight of the event occurred when Black Jack was allowed to sniff the cake and take a bite of

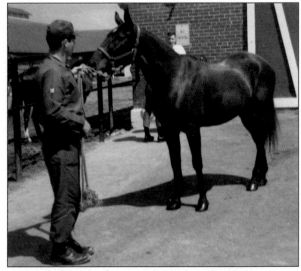

Eddie Shelton the farrier with Black Jack, 1968
Courtesy of Eddie Shelton, Fredericksburg, Virginia

Nancy Schado showing Black Jack his first birthday cake, January 19, 1968
The U.S. Army, courtesy of Nancy Schado

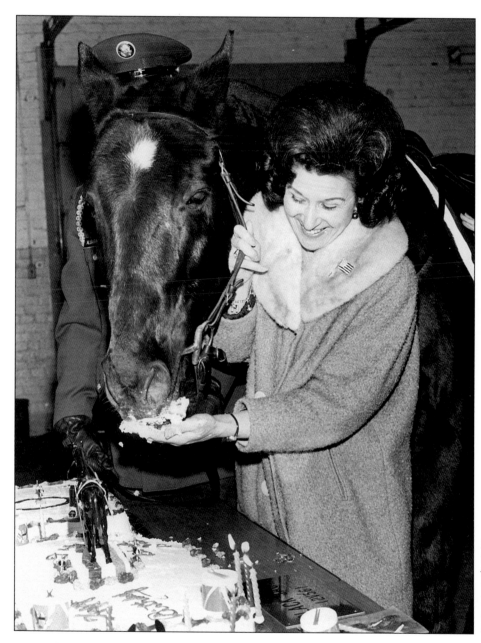

Black Jack with Nancy
Schado at his twenty-
fourth birthday party,
1971
*The U.S. Army and The
Old Guard Museum, Fort
Myer, Virginia*

Nancy Schado feeding Black Jack cake at his twenty-fifth birthday party, 1972
The U.S. Army and The Old Guard Museum, Fort Myer, Virginia

it from the serving table. A bank of photographers got pictures of him doing this and a few more of Nancy feeding her "Sweetie Pie" a piece of his birthday cake.

As a result, Black Jack's celebration was widely publicized and it became such a memorable event that Nancy decided to hold a birthday party for him every year in the future.

Another birthday celebration, 1970   *The U.S. Army and The Old Guard Museum, Fort Myer, Virginia*

Over the next four years, Black Jack's birthday parties got progressively bigger, each of them, in turn, attracting more extensive media coverage. On his twenty-fourth birthday in 1971, *The Arlington Gazette* published an article that said in part:

> How many horses get a beautiful red, white, and blue home-made cake for his birthday, plus twenty-five pounds of carrots, a bronze engraved plaque with his name and Army serial number?
>
> Maybe some of those famous race horses do, but around these parts, there is only one and that's Black Jack.

In the same article *The Gazette* also reported that Nancy Schado and the Army Arlington Ladies had adopted Black Jack. On behalf of the Caisson Platoon, CWO4 McKinney accepted Black Jack's bronze plaque and his adoption papers.

The *Army Times* also covered his 1971 party and after listing his famous accomplishments pointed out:

Children visiting the stables petting Black Jack, 1971
Courtesy of The Old Guard Caisson Platoon

> . . . Black Jack lives in semi-retirement in the stables at Fort Myer. . . . [Al]though

authorized to be retired at age twenty, Black Jack has been retained because of his historical significance. He is seen by many people who visit the stables at Fort Myer each day.

Although Black Jack was now working less than he had in his prime, he was healthy and contented, and Nancy Schado looked forward to spending many more birthdays with him in the future.

CHAPTER EIGHT

Centennial

PRIOR TO BLACK JACK'S twenty-fifth birthday party in 1972, Nancy Schado received a letter from President Nixon that read:

Dear Mrs. Schado:

Mrs. Nixon and I were glad to learn of the birthday celebration you are planning for Black Jack, and we want to join his many friends and admirers in paying tribute to him at this time.

Black Jack has been a poignant symbol of our nation's grief on many occasions over the years. Citizens in mourning felt a burst of pride in seeing this majestic horse whose quiet dignity and purpose conveyed a simpler yet deeper tribute to the memory of those heroic "riders" who have given so much for our nation.

Our people are grateful to Black Jack for helping us bear the burden of sorrow during difficult times. I know that all Americans would want to join in sending special birthday congratulations to this horse who has served our nation and our people so well.

Sincerely.
(signed) Richard Nixon

Nancy was thrilled to get President Nixon's letter, but in the back of her mind she realized that in celebrating Black Jack's twenty-fifth birthday, the beautiful horse she loved so much was now

Black Jack knocking his
cake over at his twenty-fifth
birthday party, 1972
*The U.S. Army and The Old
Guard Museum, Fort Myer,
Virginia*

well into his eighties in human terms. As she helped blow out the candles on his cake, Nancy made a fervent wish that they could celebrate many more of his birthdays together.

Then, when she presented him with his cake, Nancy said, "Aren't you going to say thank you to the people at your party?"

Black Jack whinnied with enthusiasm and proceeded to lick the cake, knocking it off the table. The crowd roared with laughter, and Black Jack raised his head with a look in his eyes that seemed to say he was having a good time, too.

At his 1973 birthday party Black Jack was still frisky and fun-loving. He put on a show eating his cake from Nancy's hands and, as he smeared his whiskers with icing, the crowd in attendance applauded with delight.

Even though Black Jack was in semi-retirement, he had been the army's choice to serve as the caparisoned horse when two other ex-presidents passed away.

An elaborate state funeral had been planned years in advance for eighty-eight year-old Harry S. Truman, the thirty-third president of the United States. When Mr. Truman was admitted to a Kansas City hospital on December 5, 1972 and his condition began to deteriorate, the army arranged to have Black Jack taken up in an airplane to prepare him for the flight to Missouri.

Black Jack's twenty-sixth birthday party, 1973. L to R: Pfc. Robert Bartel, Specialist 4 Donald Ott, Nancy Schado
The U.S. Army, Daniel Donohue

However, when Mr. Truman passed away on December 26, 1972, his widow Bess asked that her husband's funeral be kept simple. Consequently, Black Jack's services were not required for the ceremonies in Independence.

On January 22, 1973, the thirty-sixth president of the United States, Lyndon Baines Johnson, died of a heart attack at his ranch near Johnson City, Texas. The plans for his funeral called for him to lie in state at the LBJ Library in Austin, Texas, for one full day. Then his body was to be flown to Washington on January 24 to lie in state in the Capitol Rotunda.

As in the Washington procession of Herbert Hoover, Johnson's body was transported by hearse to 16th Street and Constitution Avenue, where it was transferred to a caisson for the military cortege to the Capitol Building.

To get to the transfer point, Black Jack had another long walk down the hill from Fort Myer into the city. If he was supposed to be an old and weary retiree, he certainly didn't show it during the

Portrait of Lyndon B. Johnson (1908–73), thirty-sixth president of the United States
LBJ Library, Austin, Texas, photo by Yoichi Okamoto

Black Jack beside the caisson at the transfer point on Constitution Avenue, for President Johnson's funeral, January 1973
LBJ Library, Austin, Texas, photo by Frank Wolfe

Black Jack marching in the Washington funeral for President Lyndon B. Johnson, January 1973
LBJ Library, Austin, Texas, photo by Frank Wolfe

procession to the Capitol. As usual, he tugged on the lead line most of the way and pranced along as spry as ever. And he stomped around impatiently as the pallbearers carried President Johnson's casket up the steps into the rotunda. It seemed like Black Jack had developed a behavior pattern for public appearances that he wasn't about to change.

After lying in state for eighteen hours, President Johnson's body was transported by motorcade to a church service in Washington and then to the airport for his flight home to Texas. Since the caisson and caparisoned horse were not involved in this segment of the funeral ceremonies, Black Jack's escort for the president to the Capitol was the last major funeral he worked. So it was fitting that he performed his final duties in his usual spirited manner.

After President Johnson's funeral, Black Jack seldom worked again except for the occasional funeral in Arlington National Cemetery when burials were scheduled simultaneously, requiring the use of two caparisoned horses. Although Black Jack was no longer a fixture prancing through the cemetery, he was still the object of affection for the many schoolchildren who came to visit him at the stables.

Most military horses were retired to the open pastures at Fort Meade, Maryland. However, the army, although fully aware that Black Jack was in his declining years, wanted to hold off his transfer to Fort Meade and keep him at the stables in Fort Myer. In correspondence with his

Black Jack, browning with age, and his walker, Sgt. John Best, in Arlington National Cemetery, 1972
The U.S. Army and The Old Guard Museum, Fort Myer, Virginia

superiors, the director of Army Veterinarians made the following comments about both Black Jack and Conversano Beja:

> At present, both animals are in good health and performing as required. However, this does not negate the fact that age is certainly becoming a factor. . . . Both of these animals have received considerable publicity over the years. . . . As long as both these animals are providing services in an acceptable manner, early retirement should not be considered. In the event of retirement, it is recommended that Black Jack and Conversano Beja be retired to the confines of the stables area at Fort Myer, Virginia. Fort Myer is a historic post and these horses are part of that history. Their contributions of outstanding service and the concern for their well-being in the eyes of the public, certainly warrants the respect of all concerned when their services are terminated.

With each passing year, Black Jack developed more symptoms of old age. Arthritis set in and slowed him down. He had problems with his two front feet. Eventually he required surgery on them at the University of Pennsylvania Veterinary Clinic in Philadelphia.

When the caisson soldiers tried to load Black Jack into the horse trailer for the trip to the clinic, Black Jack refused to get in. He became very difficult to handle and nothing the soldiers did seemed to help. In their frustration, they phoned Nancy Schado and asked her to come over and see what she could do.

Nancy rushed over in her car with a piece of leftover cake from her kitchen. She could see that Black Jack was adamant about not getting into the trailer, so she got in and gently called to him.

"C'mon, Sweetie Pie," she cooed. "C'mon . . . don't you want a piece of your cake?"

With little hesitation, Black Jack clumped up the ramp into the trailer. After giving him some cake and lots of kind assurance, Nancy got out of the trailer and the soldiers closed the tailgate.

As Black Jack was being hauled away, Nancy confided to Col. Harvey Perritt, who had been watching the loading process, that she was anxious about Black Jack's operation.

"I'm so afraid he's not coming back," she said.

"I wouldn't worry too much, Nancy," the colonel assured her. "He's just like the rest of The Old Guard. He's been marching too much on black top. He'll be fine. You'll see him again."

And the colonel was as good as his word. Black Jack recovered nicely and was soon back in his stall comfortably waiting for Nancy and the schoolchildren to stop by and pet him.

At his twenty-seventh birthday party, in 1974, Nancy baked his usual cake and made a little speech to

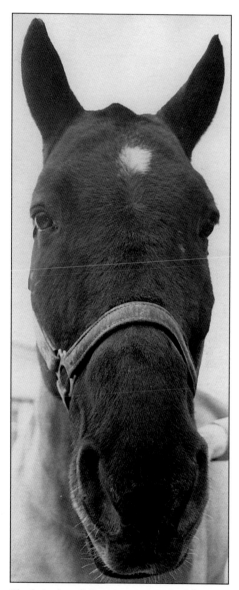

Black Jack, still handsome but aging, April 1973
The U.S. Army, courtesy of Nancy Schado

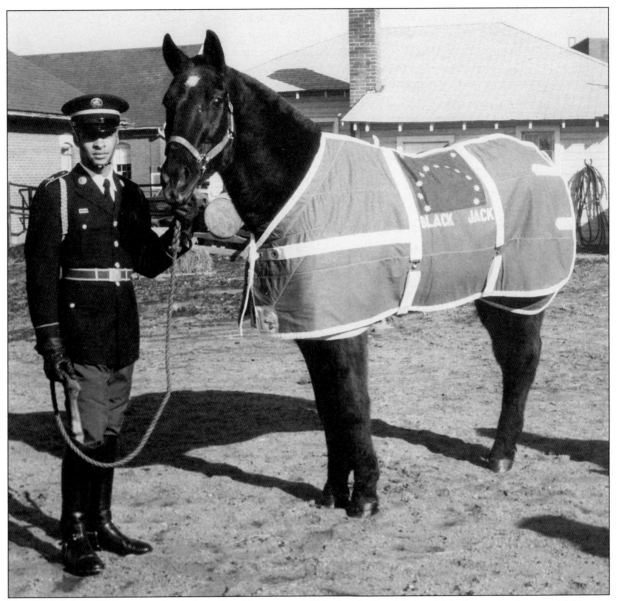

Specialist 4 Tom Chapman with Black Jack in his centennial blanket before his last birthday party, January 1976
The U.S. Army and The Old Guard Museum, Fort Myer, Virginia

the crowd in the parking lot. But Black Jack seemed tired and behaved less enthusiastically than he had at his previous birthday celebrations.

The following year, Black Jack was even less animated at his party. He was showing the first signs of kidney problems and had become quite lethargic. As the disease progressed, it was only the application of veterinary science and Nancy's and the caisson soldiers' tender loving care that kept him up and moving.

Sadly, Nancy knew their time together was limited so she went all-out for Black Jack's birthday in 1976. Because he would then be twenty-nine years old—101.5 years in human terms—the party became known as Black Jack's centennial celebration.

Nancy made arrangements to have the party in Conmy Hall across from the stables, and sent out invitations to the army authorities throughout the region. She produced photocopies of invitations that she distributed throughout the post and had stories published in the local newspapers inviting the public to attend. She also arranged the one-hour program that included special presentations for Black Jack's service to the nation.

For the occasion, Nancy used a turkey roaster and horseshoe-shaped cake pans to make him a special three-tiered, 180-pound butter pecan cake and inserted twenty-nine red, white, and blue candles around its perimeter.

Black Jack posing with his walker, Sgt. John Best, before his last birthday party, 1976

The U.S. Army and The Old Guard Museum, Fort Myer, Virginia

Black Jack at his last birthday party in Conmy Hall, 1976   *The U.S. Army, courtesy of Nancy Schado*

Urns of coffee were prepared for the adults who would attend and bowls of punch were set out for the three busloads of children brought in from local schools.

Nancy also arranged to have a distinctive centennial blanket made for Black Jack with a huge "76" emblazoned on the side. The number not only indicated the year of Black Jack's party, but it also honored the bicentennial of the nation, dating back to 1776. This was the second blanket

Nancy Schado feeds her "Sweetie Pie" his last birthday cake in Conmy Hall, 1976
The U.S. Army, courtesy of Nancy Schado

Nancy had purchased for Black Jack. The first one she bought was only two years old, but Nancy wanted him to have a brand new one for this special occasion. As an added touch, she affixed a U.S. bicentennial pin on the blanket.

When the big day arrived, Black Jack was given a thorough grooming and walked over to Conmy Hall. Inside the arena, the seats were filled with 1,500 guests and dignitaries, including the secretary of the army and the commanding general of the Military District of Washington.

When the time came to introduce Black Jack, Nancy went to the microphone and said, "Ladies and gentlemen, here is the handsomest man in the United States Army."

With that announcement, the huge door to the hall opened and a walker led the old veteran into the arena to a loud and boisterous ovation. After taking a few steps, Black Jack stopped and looked around as if he knew the party was for him. Then, as he slowly crossed the floor, the U.S. Army Band played "Happy Birthday." When Black Jack heard the music, he seemed to perk up and, as he headed for the table holding his cake and gifts, he started to tug up and down on his lead line, just as he had done on his famous walks for John Kennedy and the other great men he had followed down Constitution Avenue.

Proclamations praising his service to the country were read to the crowd. Then, when he was presented with his cake, Black Jack's eyes brightened, his ears went up, he showed his teeth, and he began moving about with a semblance of his old spirit. His behavior seemed to indicate that he knew he was basking in the spotlight of appreciation. One reporter covering the ceremony went so far as to describe Black Jack's antics as "hamming it up."

If that were the case, it was surely most appropriate. Here was a horse with over a thousand funerals to his credit; who, in his prime, averaged fifty visitors a day; who every year received Christmas cards from all over the world; and who received numerous requests for souvenirs of his horseshoes or for snippets from his tail. His reputation was so well established that one of the more popular postcards sold at Fort Myer featured his picture.

Like Man o'War, Seabiscuit, Secretariat, and the other great racehorses of the world, Black Jack had touched the peoples' hearts and won their admiration.

As the ceremony for Black Jack unfolded, Nancy Schado experienced very mixed emotions. Although she was filled with joy and pride for the horse she loved and the accolades he received, her heart ached because she knew that Black Jack's days were numbered.

"BLACK JACK"

Popular Fort Myer
post card
featuring Black
Jack
*The U.S. Army,
courtesy of Nancy
Schado*

Happy Holidays

"Black Jack" (2V56)

Nancy Schado's
Christmas card
for 1972
*The U.S. Army,
courtesy of
Nancy Schado*

Black Jack's last portrait in 1976. The "grand old man of the army"
at twenty-nine years of age—101.5 in human terms.
The U.S. Army, courtesy of Nancy Schado

CHAPTER NINE

Finale

SHORTLY AFTER Black Jack's centennial celebration, his health began to deteriorate badly. Over the next two weeks he steadily went downhill. His arthritis became more severe, and where previously he had been lethargic and showed little interest in his food, after his birthday he ate almost nothing and barely moved in his stall.

However, it was the failure of Black Jack's kidneys and liver that were causing him the most serious problems. Their dysfunction reduced the blood pressure to his brain, which adversely affected his equilibrium. To avoid being light-headed, he kept his head low and for days stood around almost motionless with his head drooped sadly to the floor. The few times Black Jack tried to lift his head, he lost his balance and stumbled around erratically.

When the soldiers of the Caisson Platoon saw him like this they were deeply disturbed. Pete Cote, the farrier, couldn't believe his eyes. In his opinion, Black Jack was the horse with the best conformation he had ever seen. Now beautiful Black Jack was just a withered shell of his former self and Pete had a difficult time accepting the pathetic transformation.

As Black Jack's condition worsened, Nancy visited him daily. It was a heart-wrenching experience for her to see him in such a forlorn state. Fearfully she kept in close contact with Pete Cote, who gave her regular reports on Black Jack's deteriorating condition.

Finally, the platoon veterinarian, Cpt. John Burns, the platoon leader, Lt. Bruce Edmiston, and the platoon sergeant, Philip Waymer, concluded that there was no longer any hope for Black Jack and the only humane thing to do was to put him down. Because Black Jack held such a position of prominence with the army, the veterinarian had to go up the chain of command to the Department of the Army to receive official permission for Black Jack's euthanasia. When the request was

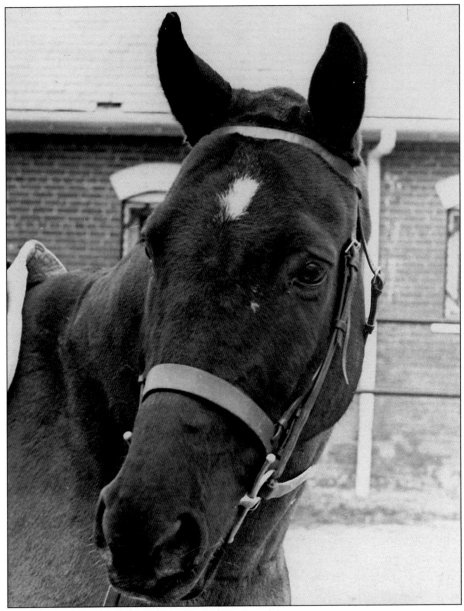

Black Jack in his final days, 1976   *The U.S. Army, courtesy of Nancy Schado*

authorized, a decision was made to have him put down as soon as possible. Considering the arrangements that had to be made, the earliest date feasible for his demise was February 6, 1976.

When Nancy heard of this decision, she was terribly upset. Sgt. Waymer attempted to relieve her apprehension by explaining that Black Jack was in pain and his condition was irreversible. Because of Black Jack's prognosis and his poor quality of life, Waymer told her it would truly be a kindness to put Black Jack out of his misery. The more Nancy considered the predicament of her poor, bedraggled horse, the more she realized that he was right.

On the evening of February 5, Nancy had her final visit with Black Jack. As always, she tried to feed him some cake; but he wasn't interested. She stroked him and talked to him, and had one

Nancy Schado visiting Black Jack for the last time on the night of February 5, 1976
Courtesy of Nancy Schado

last photograph taken with him. Then, knowing she would never see him again, she gave him a kiss and left his stall without looking back.

Before she left the barn, Pete Cote said he would phone her when the euthanasia procedure was completed. He assured her that the vet was doing the right thing, because Black Jack could survive for only a matter of hours and there was no reason for him to suffer until the very end.

The next afternoon Black Jack was under constant supervision by Cpt. Burns, Lt. Edmiston, Sgt. Waymer, and the commanders of The Old Guard and the Military District of Washington. A military policeman from Fort Myer was also on hand to observe the euthanasia process and vouch for the procedure.

Shortly after 4:30 p.m., Cpt. Burns administered a drug that heavily sedated the sick old horse. As the medication coursed through Black Jack's veins, he gently went down on his knees, then lay on his side. The veterinarian's second injection, the euthanasia drug, ended Black Jack's life.

Nancy Schado and soldiers of The Old Guard at Black Jack's interment service, 1976
The U.S. Army, courtesy of Nancy Schado

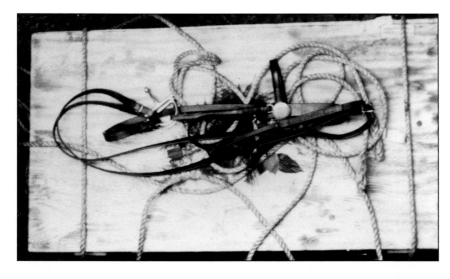

Black Jack's pine box in his grave with his bridle and Nancy Schado's flowers on top
The U.S. Army, courtesy of Nancy Schado

Under the scrutiny of the vigilant MP, all of the drug vials and paraphernalia that had been used in the euthanasia process were collected and numbered with appropriate codes for registration and storage.

Then pieces of Black Jack's hide that displayed his "US" brand and his 2V56 serial number were surgically removed. They were immediately taken to Pete Cote's forge where they were burned. This was done so that no one could steal them and claim them as prized mementos of the famous horse.

After that was accomplished, Pete Cote phoned Nancy Schado and, without going into morbid detail, advised her that Black Jack was gone. Even though Nancy knew this had to be, she cried and cried with an anguish beyond comfort. It was difficult for her to comprehend that her thirteen joyful years with Black Jack had been so swiftly relegated to the wistful realm of memory.

Back at the stables, Black Jack's carcass was loaded on a truck and, with the Fort Myer MP riding along as escort, it was transported to a special crematorium in Baltimore. Only Black Jack's tail was retained so it could be presented to Nancy Schado at a later time.

While Black Jack's remains awaited cremation in Baltimore, the fort's special platoon carpenters built a large pine box in which Black Jack's ashes were to be buried.

Amid this sad scenario, the only consolation for Nancy Schado was the fact that the army had made special plans to honor Black Jack with an unprecedented burial on the grounds of Summerall Field, the mammoth parade field at Fort Myer. The details of the funeral were

Black Jack's grave on Summerall Field with
Fort Myer Headquarters in the
background, 2000
Andy Garlatti, Windsor, Ontario

Black Jack's headstone on Summerall
Field, Fort Myer, 2000
Peter Fillman, Toronto, Ontario

publicized and invitations went out to appropriate army personnel requesting their attendance at the ceremony.

Three days after Black Jack's death, two of his stablemates, Oklahoma and Little Art, were hitched to the company's buckboard and the wagon was backed up to the barn. The pine box containing Black Jack's ashes was loaded aboard and the drivers proceeded to parade the buckboard around the post with a walker leading Raven behind. The caparison that Raven carried on his back was Black Jack's bridle.

The burial site selected on Summerall Field was located immediately behind Fort Myer Headquarters. When the buckboard crossed the parade field and arrived at the gravesite, 400 people, including dignitaries and military personnel of various ranks, were waiting to attend Black

The Commander-in-Chief's Guard marching past Black Jack's grave on Summerall Field, Fort Myer, 2000
Ray Kosi, Newport Beach, California

Jack's interment service. Standing among them in the middle of the front row closest to the grave was Nancy Schado. By this time her pain had subsided, and the tears she shed during the service were tinged as much with pride as they were with sorrow.

At the end of the service, there were a few comments by the padre; then Black Jack's bridle and Nancy's flowers were placed on top of the pine box. As Raven was led away, he stopped and

Nancy Schado with soldiers and officers of The Old Guard at the dedication of Black Jack's headstone, 1977
The U.S. Army, courtesy of Nancy Schado

stared into Black Jack's grave, and then looked back at Nancy as if he understood what had happened.

Raven's sad and curious expression captured the impact of Nancy's loss. For her, it was the end of a beautiful relationship with a truly loyal and wonderful friend.

A year after Black Jack's burial, the army held a dedication ceremony at Black Jack's grave. In appreciation for his twenty-four years of noble service to his country, they had planted a horseshoe-shaped hedge around his grave. They also had erected a granite headstone on the site with a bronze plaque to mark Black Jack's final resting place and to record his major accomplishments. No other animal who served with the U.S. Army has ever been afforded such distinction.

At the end of the dedication ceremony, Nancy posed for a photograph beside Black Jack's headstone with a group of officers and soldiers from The Old Guard. Directly behind them was the Victorian red brick building that housed Fort Myer Headquarters.

The photo depicts the most important facets of Black Jack's life: The Old Guard, Fort Myer, Nancy Schado.

The inscription on Blackjack's tombstone reads:

Black Jack – Foaled 19 January 1947
Entered 3rd US Infantry stables 22 November 1952
Retired to 3rd Infantry stables 1 June 1973
The last of the quartermaster issued horses
During his tenure as a caparisoned horse, Black Jack
Escorted the funeral caissons of Presidents
Herbert Hoover, John F. Kennedy, Lyndon B. Johnson
And General of the Army Douglas MacArthur
Died 6 February 1976

These few words on that bronze marker serve as a modest outline for the tale of a common but handsome cavalry mount who walked his way to fame and became the most illustrious horse in the history of the U.S. Army.

Pencil sketch of US–2V56, Black
Jack, that tours the country with
the U.S. Army art collection
Reuter, courtesy of Nancy Schado

Epilogue

TODAY, almost thirty years after Black Jack's death, his manicured grave is visited often by people from every walk of life who come to pay homage to his memory.

Not far away, a constant stream of visitors makes its daily pilgrimage to beautiful Arlington National Cemetery where the funerals continue to record the military history of the nation. Most recently, American victims of the fighting in Afghanistan have been buried there among their comrades from former wars. One of these was thirty-two-year-old CIA agent Johnny Michael Spann, who was murdered at the Qala-i-Jangi prison fortress by rioting Taliban captives. Another was twenty-eight-year-old Staff Sergeant Brian Prosser of the Army Special Forces Command, tragically killed by friendly fire.

Much of the information I received on Arlington National Cemetery was supplied by Barbara Owens, Public Affairs Specialist with the U.S. Army Military District of Washington. She devoted two days from her hectic schedule to give me and my associates an enlightening personal tour of the cemetery and Fort Myer. She also put me in touch with Warren G. Miller, a photographer/historian from Kensington, Maryland, who has a personal collection of 22,000 photos of Arlington National Cemetery. Mr. Miller was kind enough to let me choose from his collection to enhance the merits of this book. I sincerely appreciate his generous cooperation and assistance.

At Fort Myer, the current demands on the Caisson Platoon are as arduous as ever. Consequently, the complement at the stables today has been increased to forty-one horses. Their duties remain constant; only their names have changed. Some of the black horses working the funerals today are Lee, Grant, Dunn, Bucky, Buddy and Mike. Some of the grays are Spider, Andalusia, Steele, Judy, Ballerina, Bonnie, and Babe. The present caparisoned horse is Sergeant

President Kennedy's grave with Arlington House in the distance. Gen. Sheridan's lone tombstone can be seen on the lawn to the right of the mansion.

Warren G. Miller, Kensington, Maryland

The author and his research/photographic team at the Iwo Jima monument adjacent to Arlington National Cemetery, 2000. L to R: Andy Garlatti, Peter Fillman, Bob Knuckle, Ray Kosi, Charlie Hickey

Barbara Owens and CWO5 Charles Sowles in front of the caisson stable, 2002. Between them is Sergeant York, Black Jack's latest and most promising successor at Fort Myer.

Warren G. Miller, Kensington, Maryland

York, who has been at the stables for the last six years. The alternate "cap" horse is Nick. Before them, the riderless horses included Smokey, Danny Boy, and Palo Alto, often referred to as "BJ Jr.," because he so resembled Black Jack.

All of these horses have their own beauty and charm, but it's difficult to imagine that any of them will ever attain the fame of Black Jack.

After Black Jack died, the Caisson Platoon kept his stall free and used it as a museum to honor his memory. More recently, they have expanded the size of the museum by converting the caisson room into a space where visitors can view Black Jack's photos, his medical records, other artifacts such as his halter, a bit, his currycomb and brush, and his 1976 centennial blanket. Dr. Harry Rozmiarek, the former attending veterinarian at Fort Myer, plans to donate the horseshoes Black Jack wore in President Kennedy's funeral to the museum for display. He received the shoes from the platoon farrier immediately after the president's burial and has kept them in storage at his home ever

Walking in Black Jack's footsteps. Sgt. Jason Adler and "cap" horse Danny Boy, 1998.
The U.S. Army, courtesy of The Old Guard

since. Dr. Rozmiarek is now professor and chief of Laboratory Animal Medicine at the University of Pennsylvania in Philadelphia. He was most generous in sharing his memories of Black Jack, as well as many anecdotes from his time at Fort Myer.

On the wall of the new museum there is a framed copy of President Nixon's letter praising Black Jack's service to the nation. The museum also has two caissons on display. Standing outside

Col. Stanley Bonta and Maj. Gen. Robert Arter unveiling Black Jack's portrait for the museum at The Old Guard stables, 1977
The U.S. Army, courtesy of Nancy Schado

the entrance is a gray, life-size replica of a Civil War period cavalry officer's horse.

The only member of the Caisson Platoon still at the stables who actually worked with Black Jack is Pete Cote, the farrier. His recollections of those days were very helpful to me in writing this book.

The present Caisson Platoon leader, CWO5 Charles Sowles, was also most accommodating. During the course of several personal interviews and countless telephone conversations, he supplied a great deal of valuable information and put me in touch with a number of people who had stories to tell about Black Jack. First and foremost among those contacts is Nancy Schado.

A widow since 1983, Nancy lives alone in West Chester, Ohio, about twenty miles north of Cincinnati. From the first time I spoke with her on the telephone she was most gracious and willing to assist in my project. Nancy told me she had a trunk full of newspaper clippings and photos of Black Jack and said she was willing to share them with me if I covered the cost of having them reproduced. In order to see what she had, and in my desire to interview her in person, I took a motor trip to West Chester with my photographer, Andy Garlatti, and Ray Kosi, one of my research associates.

When we got to her condo in West Chester, I was astounded at the wealth of information she had at her disposal. Nancy allowed me to select the articles I wanted from her vast collection but wanted me to take the material to a photographic lab in Cincinnati to have the pictures reproduced. I didn't object to her suggestion, but realized that such a process would take a number of days. This would have made things difficult for both me and my companions, who had other demands on their time.

Somehow over the course of our interview, Nancy changed her mind and agreed that I could take away the actual photos and documents as long as I took good care of them and promised to return them as soon as I was finished with them.

Dr. Harry Rozmiarek, 2001
Courtesy of Dr. Harry Rozmiarek

Pete Cote, the farrier, at work at the Fort Myer stables, 2001
Courtesy of Pete Cote

Nancy Schado with the little black horse figurine she used for all of Black Jack's birthday cakes, 2001   *Peter Fillman, Toronto, Ontario*

If the readers of this book think that Nancy's devotion to a horse, even a famous one like Black Jack, seems peculiar, Nancy herself would not disagree. She told me, "You don't have to be crazy to do the things I did, but it helps."

However, I think it's more accurate to say that Nancy is a vigorous woman with intense and varied interests. She has always pushed herself to keep busy and insists, "There's nothing worse than a boring life—Lord, no."

Seeing Nancy's apartment helped me to understand what makes her such a vibrant character. The walls of her living room are lined with mementos, not only those of Black Jack, but with all sorts of memorabilia she has collected over the years.

A large, framed portrait of Abraham Lincoln dominates one wall. That's because Nancy was born in Springfield, Illinois, which is also where Lincoln is buried. Hanging close to Lincoln's portrait is a signed and dedicated photo from Gen. Colin L. Powell taken when he was chairman of the Joint Chiefs of Staff. Over her dining room table is a large painting of Civil War Confederate general Nathan Bedford Forrest astride his white charger, King Philip.

Every available surface in her dining room and living room is covered with knick-knacks and expensive figurines of varying shapes and sizes.

Because Nancy is a Civil War buff, she has collected a host of souvenirs from that conflict, including cannonballs from the Battle of Gettysburg. The hallway leading to her washroom features several photos showing the hanging of the conspirators who assassinated Lincoln. Her spare bedroom is piled high with Civil War memorabilia that includes buttons, pins, maps, charts, and infantry rosters dated from that time as well as a black pot-bellied stove that is over one hundred years old. Although the mass of material in the room appears to be jumbled and disorganized, I'm sure an auctioneer of authentic historical artifacts would quickly assess its value to be a veritable gold mine.

Of course the mementos of Black Jack are everywhere—on the walls, in the halls, over doorways, in the kitchen. On prominent display atop one cabinet is the little black horse figurine that she once used to decorate Black Jack's birthday cakes. Hanging above the entrance to her pantry is a professionally lettered sign declaring that area to be "Black Horse Alley."

Even though she has surrounded herself with this eclectic museum of memories, it wasn't Nancy's peculiarity that overwhelmed me; it was her enthusiasm for her wide variety of interests. As she led me through her life story and her experiences with Black Jack, I was mesmerized by her zest for life and by her boundless devotion to the things and people she loves. Equally impressive is her remarkable memory of events that happened so long ago.

Photographs from those times show that she was a tiny, attractive woman with an engaging smile. Even though she is now seventy-six, Nancy is still petite and pretty. Well-groomed with auburn hair, she dresses fashionably and has maintained her wonderful sense of humor. Her only concession to time is that, plagued by arthritis in her back and knees, she uses a cane to walk.

Her love of horses has never diminished. When she lost her third husband in 1983, she had him buried at Arlington National Cemetery and was given the privilege of choosing all-black horses from the Caisson Platoon for his funeral.

Most amazingly she says when she dies she wants to be cremated and have her ashes buried in a cookie tin beside Black Jack on Summerall Field. Not only did she show me the red, white, and blue cookie tin emblazoned with stars and stripes that is to be used, she feels sure that her wishes in this regard will be fulfilled.

Nancy Schado with the cookie tin for her ashes that she hopes to have buried beside Black Jack, 2001

Andy Garlatti, Windsor, Ontario

Nancy Schado with her West Highland Terrier Nancy Joe

Ray Kosi, Newport Beach, California

"I know the army engineers can make this happen," she assured me.

Nancy's family must wonder about this odd request. She has one daughter living nearby and two sons, both of whom have served in the military. Her children have given her three grandchildren and seven great-grandchildren, whom she sees quite regularly. The baby she tenderly cares for now is her West Highland terrier, Nancy Joe. Nevertheless, she insists on being buried beside Black Jack.

As I was leaving with a satchel full of her most prized possessions, the last thing Nancy said to me was, "I hope your book makes Black Jack more famous than he already is."

Finding Arthur A. Carlson was a difficult task. The only information I had on him was the fact that he lived in Mobile, Alabama. When I tried to get his phone number from long-distance information, I was informed that it was unlisted. I tried every possible way I could think of to ascertain his number but was unsuccessful.

Then I heard that a freelance writer in Texas had done a piece on Arlington National Cemetery for the *Dallas Morning News* in which she had quoted Arthur Carlson extensively. When I telephoned the writer, she was polite and supportive, but because she found Arthur to be a rather reserved and private person, she didn't feel she could give me his phone number without his permission. She said she would telephone Arthur and get back to me.

Time went by and I didn't hear from her so I began investigating other avenues to contact Arthur directly. I even went so far as to make an inquiry about hiring the services of a private detective. Because his rates were prohibitive, I decided to hold off using him until I had exhausted all other possibilities.

Finally, I made a phone call to the Mobile Chamber of Commerce. Nobody there knew anything about Arthur Carlson, but with some prompting, they found his address and phone number listed in the city directory.

Prior to phoning Arthur, I was anxious. One entire chapter in my book was to be written presenting the Kennedy funeral through Arthur Carlson's eyes. If he was such a private person, I was concerned that he very well might be offended by my prying into his affairs and refuse to talk to me. However, when I did reach him at home one evening, I found him to be one of the most courteous and cooperative persons I have ever interviewed. The information he gave me and the memories he shared were beyond my expectations.

The first few years after the Kennedy funeral Arthur used to receive about ten inquiries annually from various sources. More recently they have dwindled to one or two a year. He said very few people he meets now know about his walk with Black Jack in John Kennedy's funeral, and he makes a point not to tell them about that experience in his life because he thinks that might sound like he is bragging. But Arthur added that his wife tells everyone she meets.

Arthur is retired from his long-time occupation of working in instrumentation on the oil rigs in the Gulf of Mexico. He lives in Mobile with his wife Pat. Their one daughter, Shawna, was recently married in Ireland and resides with her husband in California.

Although Pete Duda was gone from Fort Myer when Black Jack died, he said he cried when he heard the news of his death. After Pete left the army, he worked for Eastern Airlines, served twenty-one years with the Fairfax County Police Department, and for the last seventeen years has been a successful real estate agent in Alexandria, Virginia. Pete and his wife Kay have three daughters who have added four grandchildren to their family.

Eddie Shelton, one of the farriers at Fort Myer, left the army in 1968. Ever since then he has plied his trade as a blacksmith, traveling with his mobile unit to forty-five different farms spread throughout Stafford County, in central Virginia.

"This is horse country," he said. "There's lots to do here in central Virginia and the work keeps me busy."

In the course of a year, on a rotating basis, he shoes and trims 450 animals including horses, ponies and mules. Eddie lives with his wife Rebecca on their 204-acre farm outside historic Fredericksburg, Virginia. As a hobby, he plows and rakes hay on his land the old-fashioned way, with teams of mules or horses.

In obtaining photos for this book, I dealt with numerous contacts at various libraries, agencies, military institutes, and archives. Providing the pictures to me was a laborious process for

Arthur Carlson, 2001
Courtesy of Arthur Carlson

Pete Duda, 2001
Courtesy of Pete Duda

Pfc. Pete Duda with Black Jack, 1959
Courtesy of Pete Duda

them. They gathered a sample of appropriate photos, photocopied them, and sent the photocopies to me for my selection. Then I ordered the photos by their identification numbers, and my order was processed and mailed back to me. Every organization I worked with was supportive and most helpful in finding meaningful photographs that would supplement my text. Some of the oldest and most historic photographs I was able to obtain were of Fort Reno.

Several of these came from the Fort Reno Visitor Center, a museum and interpretive center that was opened in 1997. Other historic pictures of the old fort came from the Carnegie Library in nearby El Reno. Although Fort Reno is no longer a military base, there is a plan in progress to restore many of its historic buildings. So far, the fort's hospital, officers' quarters, commissary, and chapel have been renovated. This is the same chapel that was built by the German prisoners of war in 1944. Some twenty other buildings of historic significance are destined for renovation in the future.

A large number of priceless photos were supplied by the John F. Kennedy Library in Boston; others were received from the Military History Institute Archives in Carlisle, Pennsylvania. A few came from the collections of professional photographers such as Ken Poch of Reston, Virginia, and Jim Friedman of Bedford Heights, Ohio.

Luwanda McKinney, a daughter of CWO4 John McKinney, also supplied several valuable photos of her father as well as some anecdotes about his experiences with the Caisson Platoon.

CWO4 John McKinney riding at his retirement parade on Conversano Beja, Summerall Field, May, 1974. Beside him is a caisson soldier riding Harvey P. named after Col. Harvey H. Perritt Jr., the commander of The Old Guard at the time.
Courtesy of the McKinney family

Because Chief McKinney was responsible for organizing the funerals of Presidents Kennedy, Hoover, Johnson, Eisenhower, and General MacArthur, he played a pivitol role in Black Jack's rise to fame.

Mr. McKinney's work in President Kennedy's funeral earned him the Army Commendation Medal for *"enhancing the stature and prestige of the United States and the military service at national and international levels during the state funeral of President John F. Kennedy."*

In an army career that spanned thirty-three years, Chief McKinney served fifteen of those years – from 1959 to 1974 – as the leader of the Caisson Platoon. The stables at Fort Myer are now named in John McKinney's honor, and his reputation as an honest, forthright, and amiable commander is deeply etched in the memories of the men who served with him.

Epilogue

When Chief McKinney retired, he moved his wife and two youngest children back to his roots in Polk County, North Carolina, where he purchased a small farm and continued to pursue his life-long passion of working with horses. After thirteen years at his farm, John McKinney passed away at the untimely age of 68 years. It is most fitting that he was buried with full military honors in his beloved Arlington National Cemetery, section 35, tomb marker number 1711, just a short distance from the Tomb of the Unknowns where members of his cherished army unit, The Old Guard, maintain their constant vigil.

In closing, I must say that I owe a debt of gratitude to all the people who contributed photographs and anecdotes for this book. Their assistance has been invaluable in helping me tell the story of Black Jack, who surely belongs on the historic roster of famous horses that grace the annals of American history.

A sampling of these memorable steeds includes the following:

Baldy	Ridden by Gen. George Meade during the Civil War
Black Tom	Col. Charles May, War with Mexico
Blueskin	Gen. George Washington, Revolutionary War
Cincinnati	Gen. Ulysses S. Grant, Civil War
Comanche	Capt. Myles Keogh, Indian Wars
Jeff	Gen. John J. Pershing, World War I
Kidron	Gen. John J. Pershing, World War I
King Philip	Gen. Nathan B. Forrest, Civil War
Little Sorrel	Gen. Stonewall Jackson, Civil War
Old Bob	Abraham Lincoln
Rienzi	Gen. Philip H. Sheridan, Civil War
Traveller	Gen. Robert E. Lee, Civil War
Vic	Gen. George Custer, Battle of the Little Big Horn

Although Black Jack never went into battle like most of these famous horses, I think it's fair to say that the legacy of his service to the nation is comparable to any of them.

And surely Black Jack's rise from obscurity to fame is a wonderful success story to stir the imagination and warm the hearts of readers of all ages, everywhere.

Black Jack and Pfc. Arthur A. Carlson, the famous pair that walked their way to fame in November 1963
The U.S. Army

Acknowledgements

The author gratefully acknowledges the assistance of the following individuals in the preparation and publication of this book:

Judy Allen, Lyndon B. Johnson Library and Museum, Austin, Texas
CPT Janis Baker, Veterinarian, Fort Myer, Virginia
Ernie Bomhoff, El Reno, Oklahoma
Alan Bogan, Curator, The Old Guard Museum, Fort Myer, Virginia
Larry Bleiberg, Travel Editor, *Dallas Morning News*, Dallas, Texas
Joan Caron, Kunhardt Productions, New York, NY
MSG Greg Corcoran, U.S. Army Band "Pershing's Own," Fort Myer, Virginia
Pete Cote, Fredericksburg, Maryland
Sharon Culley, U.S. National Archives, College Park, Maryland
William J. Davis, General Douglas MacArthur Foundation, Norfolk, Virginia
Jim Detlefsen, Herbert Hoover Presidential Library, West Branch, Iowa
Pete Duda, Pfc 3rd U.S. Infantry Regiment, Alexandria, Virginia
Debbie Elmenhorst, El Reno Carnegie Library, El Reno, Oklahoma
James Enos, Photographer, Carlisle, Pennsylvania
Patricia Flynn, Alfred A. Knopf Publishing Co., New York, New York
Bill Fowler, Consultant, Dundas, Ontario
Jim Friedman, Photographer, Bedford Heights, Ohio
Tim Gordon, General Store Publishing House, Burnstown, Ontario
Randy Hackenburg, U.S. Army Military Institute, Carlisle, Pennsylvania
Luther Hanson, Curator, Quartermaster Museum, Fort Lee, Virginia
Margaret Harman, Audiovisual Archives, Lyndon Baines Johnson Library, Austin, Texas
Kim Holien, Historian, Fort Myer, Virginia
Rosemary Kenopic, General Store Publishing House, Burnstown, Ontario
Larry Ketron, Visual Information, Fort Detrick, Maryland
SSG Ward Lacey, Caisson Platoon, Fort Myer, Virginia

Marty Marten, Cedar Vale, Kansas
Dr. Herman Mayeux, Director, Fort Reno Research Service, U.S. Department of Agriculture
Robert Melhorn, U.S. Army Public Affairs, Washington, D.C.
CWO5 Jeanne Pace, The Old Guard Fife and Drum Corps, Fort Myer, Virginia
Ken Poch, Photographer, Reston, Virginia
John Rives, Comprint Military Publications, Gaithersburg, Maryland
Dr. Harry Rozmiarek, University of Pennsylvania Veterinary School
Philip Scott, Lyndon B. Johnson Library and Museum, Austin, Texas
Linda Seelke, Lyndon B. Johnson Library and Museum, Austin, Texas
Eddie Shelton, Fredericksburg, Maryland
Gayle L. Stewart, Spicewood, Texas
Robert Tissing, Lyndon B. Johnson Library and Museum, Austin, Texas
Sgt. John Turpen, U.S. Army Band "Pershing's Own," Fort Myer, Virginia
Sharon Walker, Public Affairs, Fort Myer, Virginia
Dan Warren, Warren's Studio, El Reno, Oklahoma
Sgt. Jamelle Wyman, Public Affairs, The Old Guard, Fort Myer, Virginia
Sgt. Michael Yoder, The U.S. Army Band "Pershing's Own," Fort Myer, Virginia
Jim Zobel, MacArthur Memorial Library and Archives, Norfolk, Virginia

The author gratefully acknowledges the cooperation and assistance of the following institutions and publications in the preparation and publication of this book:

The Alexandria Gazette, Alexandria, Virginia
The Arkansas City Traveler, Arkansas City, Kansas
Arlington National Cemetery, Arlington, Virginia
Army Times, Springfield, Virginia
Comprint Military Publications, Gaithersburg, Maryland
The Dallas Morning News, Dallas, Texas
El Reno Carnegie Library, El Reno, Oklahoma
El Reno Tribune, El Reno, Oklahoma
The Old Guard Museum, Fort Myer, Virginia
Fort Reno Visitor Center, Fort Reno, Oklahoma

Acknowledgements

Hamilton Public Library, Hamilton, Ontario
The Hamilton Spectator, Hamilton, Ontario
Herbert Hoover Presidential Library, West Branch, Iowa
John F. Kennedy Library, Boston, Massachusetts
Kunhardt Productions, New York, New York
Lyndon Baines Johnson Library and Museum, Austin, Texas
MacArthur Memorial Library and Archives, Norfolk, Virginia
McMaster University Library, Hamilton, Ontario
Mobile Alabama Chamber of Commerce
The Pentagram News, Fort Myer, Virginia
Quartermaster Museum, Fort Lee, Virginia
Random House of Canada, Toronto, Ontario
San Antonio Express, San Antonio, Texas
Toronto Star, Toronto, Ontario
U.S. Army Military District of Washington, Fort McNair, D.C.
U.S. Army Military History Institute, Carlisle, Pennsylvania
U.S. Army Public Affairs, Fort Myer, Virginia
U.S. National Archives, College Park, Maryland
Warren's Studio, El Reno, Oklahoma
The Washington Post, Washington, D.C.

Special thanks to the following individuals for the time and effort they spent in assisting the author with the preparation and publication of this book:

Arthur Carlson, Pfc 3rd U.S. Infantry Regiment, The Old Guard, Mobile, Alabama
Diane Costin, Librarian, El Reno Carnegie Library, El Reno, Oklahoma
Allan Goodrich, Archivist, John F. Kennedy Library and Museum, Boston, Massachusetts
Jane Karchmar, my editor, General Store Publishing House, Burnstown, Ontario
Elizabeth Knuckle, associate writer, researcher, data processor, Dundas, Ontario
Warren G. Miller, visual history photographer, Kensington, Maryland
Barbara Owens, Public Affairs, U.S. Army Military District of Washington
Nancy Schado, West Chester, Ohio

CWO5 Charles Sowles, The Old Guard Caisson Platoon, Fort Myer, Virginia
Connie Hart Yellowman, Fort Reno Visitor Center, Oklahoma
The author's research/photographic team:

>Peter Fillman, Toronto, Ontario
>Andy Garlatti, Windsor, Ontario
>Charles Hickey, Essex, Ontario
>Ray Kosi, Newport Beach, California

INDEX

ABOUT THE AUTHOR

Robert Knuckle is an actor, public speaker, and award-winning writer for stage, radio, and television. His play *I Am Not a Legend*, based on the life of renowned Green Bay Packer football coach Vince Lombardi, has been performed on the stage at many venues, including the Edinburgh Festival, network radio, and ESPN television. In all these presentations, Mr. Knuckle played the part of Vince Lombardi.

Mr. Knuckle is also the author of five historical books and one book for children. His avid interest in President Kennedy and the celebrated horses of the Caisson Platoon at Arlington National Cemetery inspired him to research and write this story of Black Jack, the famous riderless horse.